View from LeConte

View from LeConte

Memoirs
of a
Cold-War
Diplomat

Ralph Stokes Collins

Grandson Christopher Robert Mann, born 1984, with Grandpa.

Dedication

To the beloved grandchildren and great-grandchildren of

Ralph and Maria Collins

When Grandpa Ralph wrote his autobiography in 1987-88, it consisted of 60 typewritten pages of text with no pictures and little background information.

In order to give you the context for Grandpa Ralph's work and the times he lived in, we have added photographs, maps, and letters. His son Randall Collins has prepared descriptions of the political situations in which he worked. Other family members have contributed sidebars and letters.

May this book give you a better understanding of the breadth of his experiences and encourage you to take your own great steps forward.

Grandchildren

Lindsay Collins Olesberg
Adrian Keith Wagner
Alan Gerard Wagner
Anthony McConnell-Collins
Maren Diane McConnell-Collins Long
Christopher Robert Mann

Great-grandchildren

Michael Collins Olesberg
Mary Bryson Olesberg
Maxime Ulysse Altaï Min Perrin-Wagner
Taylor Rose Mann

And others yet to come....

Returning home to Ayden from the University of North Carolina.

Contents

Stalin's presence loomed in post-war Berlin.

Becoming a cold-war diplomat

Dad's love of the German language and his affinity for foreign languages in general led him onto paths he could not have foreseen when he was a youngster growing up in North Carolina farm country.

Dad's fluency in German and his spirit of adventure led him into foreign service in Germany as World War II was ending.

In 1948 we left Berlin as the Western powers began the Berlin air lift. This heroic event was the West's response to Soviet efforts to swallow Berlin and eventually all of Western Europe.

The Communist threat was huge, and Dad's diplomatic career was shaped in response to that threat. He went to Columbia University to learn Russian. To quote a letter to him from the US Foreign Service Institute,

"....there is no question but that those people who are specializing on the Soviet Union will be working for the entire foreseeable future on problems at the core of American foreign relations."

Erica

Alum Bluff Cave on the trail to Mt. LeConte.

Conquering mountains

In Dad's own words, "In 1987, I hiked up LeConte for the 100th time. It is my favorite hike, and I hope to continue hiking it for a long time. In fact, I like the symbolism of conquering mountains."

Dad did not elaborate on the symbolism of conquering mountains. He didn't have too – that is how he lived his life. Every mountain – all his life – he took it on and conquered it.

For me, Mt. LeConte is a place that Dad loved to take anyone who would go with him, and I can continue his legacy by taking family and friends on a hike up Mt. LeConte.

For those descendants who don't know Mt. LeConte – they may ask their parent or grandparent – who will know – to relate the stories of what it was like to walk with the man who perhaps didn't verbalize everything but who had so much to say.

Melissa

A long climb and a great view

Ralph Collins spent a lot of time reading while growing up on the farm in North Carolina, so much so that he skipped two grades in elementary school and graduated from high school at age 16. He was the first child in his family of ten to attend college.

Ralph's family was proud when he enrolled in the University of North Carolina at Chapel Hill. There he developed a love for German language and literature which led him to spend a year in Germany after college and to pursue a PhD in German at Johns Hopkins University after he returned to the States.

He decided to pursue a career in teaching and found a position teaching German and French at Maryville College in eastern Tennessee. His chosen career path, however, was to take an unexpected turn.

As World War II drew to a close, the US Department of State urgently needed Americans who were fluent in German to assist with the collection of German documents as the war ended. While attending a meeting of the Modern Language Association in Washington DC in December 1944, Ralph heard about the need and decided to respond. His wife Maria encouraged him to apply.

Ralph was hired. Within three months he was sent to London and Versailles for training and orientation to a job that would eventually lead him into the Foreign Service.

He performed so well and was so adept at languages that the State Department sent him to Columbia University for a year to learn Russian and then assigned him to the US Embassy in Moscow. In addition to German and Russian, he was proficient in French, Italian, and Spanish.

Ralph enjoyed immensely his time in the diplomatic service, but after 22 years he decided to go back to college teaching. He returned to Maryville College, where he and Maria became very active in the community.

This is Ralph's story.

Map of eastern North Carolina.

North Carolina

1910-1932

Ralph's parents, James Hanrahan Collins and Margaret Melissa Stokes Collins, with their oldest son, John Arthur, born October 19, 1899.

Growing up in farm country

My birth certificate says that I was born alive at 11 p.m. November 1, 1910, when my father, James Hanrahan Collins, was 35 and my mother, Margaret Melissa Stokes Collins, was 33. The place of residence was Grifton, Pitt County, NC RFD. I was born at home, about 7 miles from Grifton. The attending physician, Dr. William Cobb Whitford, resided in Grifton.

My father had acquired the farm in 1901, and I lived my first seven years there. The house no longer stands, and I do not have a clear mental picture of it. I remember three things about it: a fireplace, a room with a piano, and, vaguely, the kitchen. We usually bathed in a tub in the kitchen, but I remember also bathing in a tub behind the house in warm weather.

I remember the fields, most vividly the cane field, which I think my father had only one year. But the operation of the pressing of the juice and the cooking of the molasses is one of my most vivid memories of that place. I remember riding with my older brothers, with a wagon-load of watermelons, to Shelmerdine. I remember catching some perch in a small stream and my brothers catching pike in a swamp behind the farm.

Our cousin, Thomas Stokes, who was born in 1901, tells how he and my oldest brother, Arthur, played together. Arthur had a bicycle and was teaching Tom how to ride it. Tom fell off the bicycle into a little ditch. He had to change into some of Arthur's clothes until he could get back home. He felt very embarrassed about wearing Arthur's clothes.

Birthplace of Ralph's father, James Hanrahan Collins.

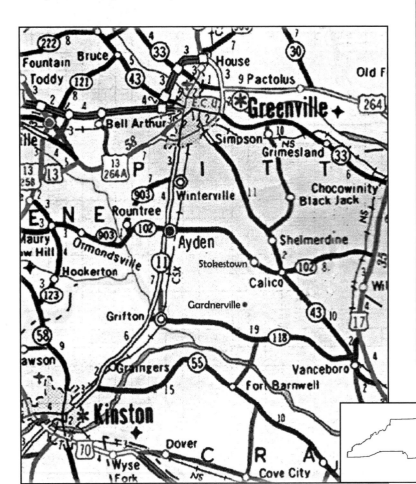

James Hanrahan Collins' parents named him after James Hanrahan, the Irishman who ran the store at Hanrahan's Crossroads, 5 miles south of Ayden.

James' father, Randall Parrott Collins, fought in the Confederate army and was a prisoner of war at Johnson's Island, near Sandusky, Ohio. Ralph Collins liked to tell the story of how Randall, while a soldier, stopped to ask for a drink of water at the home of Horace Ives, in Pitt County, North Carolina.

After the Civil War ended, Randall returned to Pitt County and married Sarah Rebecca Ives, the girl who had given him the drink of water. He went to work in Mr. Hanrahan's store. James Hanrahan Collins, Ralph's father, was born in 1875.

Erica Collins

Aside from the farm, what I remember best is Timothy Church, located about a mile west of our home, at Gardner's Crossroads, now Gardnerville. I remember the annual church picnic, or homecoming, under the trees in the churchyard. The Gardner home was on the other side of the road from the church.

Timothy Christian Church, built in 1894.

Around the corner, to the north, was the small schoolhouse where I went to school, probably for two years. I remember also going to Vanceboro, to the east, where my oldest brother, Arthur, worked in a bank. I remember riding to see our grandmother at Uncle Tom Stokes' house. At first we rode in a buggy, but later in a car. We also visited other aunts, uncles, and cousins: Stokeses and Moores. We also went to Ayden from time to time. My parents bought me clothes at the Turnage Store in Ayden.

In 1918, when I was 7, we moved to a farm about 2 miles east of Ayden proper. Our home near Ayden was much larger. I slept mainly in the downstairs back bedroom, sharing a bed with a brother. We had a large dining room and kitchen. Water came from a pump on the back porch. There was no indoor plumbing, only a pump on the back entrance-way. The outhouse was back of the barn. Only later, when we moved into Ayden about 1928, did we have real plumbing.

There were large barns for the mules and the farm machinery, large pack-houses for the tobacco, and barns for corn and hay. On the left side of the path (road) from the house, through the fields to the woods, there were four curing barns for the tobacco. There were three houses for the black tenant farmers.

Ralph in sixth grade, in 1923.

There was always work to do, and every member of the family stayed busy. I too worked in

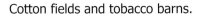
Cotton fields and tobacco barns.

Hauling tobacco to the barn.

Some people carried drawstring pouches of loose tobacco and rolled their own cigarettes. Not Grand-daddy Collins [Ralph's father]. He smoked unfiltered Wings cigarettes. His fingers were stained yellow from smoking; he always had a cigarette between his fingers.

Myrtle Ruth Thomas (Ralph's niece)

Ralph's mother, Margaret Collins, was one of the smartest women and very productive. She was always doing something, from gardening to crocheting. She and her daughter Thelma did all the cooking for the family, hired hands, and tenant farmers. The big meal was served at noon. The tobacco gatherers used to say that Margaret's cornbread tasted like cake.

Irma Belle Morris (Ralph's sister-in-law)

In the old days it was popular to have large families in order to have help on the farm. Grand-daddy Collins gave his children tasks to do every day. Ralph was usually found sitting under a tree reading a book. When school started, all the children gravitated to Ralph for help with their homework.

Raymond L. Collins, Jr. (Ralph's nephew)

When minstrel shows came to Greenville, they performed in a tent or a tobacco warehouse. Billy Sunday came and held revivals. The collection was put in washtubs at the front of the tent.

John Arthur Collins II (Ralph's nephew)

the fields of tobacco, cotton, and corn. I had certain chores, like taking the milk-cow to the pasture. I never milked her – that was usually the job of my next older brother. Also a few times I picked cotton.

During the tobacco harvesting season, I usually "handed" tobacco – that is, I picked up bunches of three or four leaves and handed them to the tyer, who looped the tobacco onto sticks, which were then hung in the curing barns. On days we were not harvesting, I helped sucker the tobacco plants in the fields.

We boys liked to be allowed to spend the night at the curing barns now and then. We slept on make-shift beds under the barn shelters. When we awakened in the middle of the night, it was fun to see the fires glowing in the barn furnaces.

Sunday dinners were usually festive occasions, with relatives or friends visiting us. There was always plenty to eat, and my older sisters helped my mother prepare the food. Estelle, our oldest sister, played the piano, and we all liked to listen, and sometimes we sang together as she played. The boys played games – baseball or marbles. On Saturday afternoons we usually went to town, visited around, and went to the movies. We always went to church on Sunday.

Because it was about two miles to town, we usually rode to school, mostly by car, but sometimes we had to walk home. I enjoyed school. I remember an occasion, probably in third grade, when the teacher said I had copied something from another pupil, but I think it must have been the other way around. I believe that was my first year in the Ayden school.

I liked to read a lot, and frequently took library books home. Some of my classmates probably thought I was a regular book-worm. Anyhow, I did

Harvesting and eating watermelon.

My grandparents (Ralph's parents) had dinners for all the tobacco warehousers and buyers from Liggett & Myers, Reynolds, and other tobacco companies. The guests numbered around 200. They were served stew which was cooked outside over a big fire in cast-iron laundry pots. Grandpa kept tasting it and saying it was never hot enough, so he added red pepper. The women at the house prepared trays of pastry dough which they cut into squares and cooked in the stew, like dumplings.

When tobacco was sold, Grandpa Collins set Rosa, his youngest daughter, on top of the pile of tobacco. She was all dressed up and real pretty. He'd call out, "Here's Collins tobacco!" The newspaper reported that Collins tobacco sold for $1 per pound. Most other tobacco sold for 80¢ per pound.

Uncle Jim Ed lived next door to the tobacco warehouse and went there each evening to watch the weighing of the tobacco. He said one tobacco buyer carried a different brand of cigarette in each pocket so he could smoke the brand of whichever buyer he was with on any given day. Cigar wrappers were made from pretty leaves without holes.

Everyone pitched in on the task of "handing" tobacco. Those on the left side hand leaves to those on the right, who tie the leaves in bunches. The woman in right foreground hangs the bunches on the rack, which will be taken to the drying barn.

Tobacco

As told by

John Arthur Collins II

Tobacco auction in the 1910s.

Hog killing in 1920s.

Hogs on the hoof. A mature hog can easily weigh several hundred pounds.

In the kettles the fat is being rendered for lard for cooking. The farm was self-sufficient except for a few staples such as salt, sugar, and coffee.

well at school and made good grades. The principal allowed me to skip the seventh grade altogether. I must have skipped another grade earlier, because I graduated from Ayden High School in 1926 in the same class as Raymond, my next older brother. In my Senior year I participated in a state-wide math contest and was rated highest in the state. That was a happy moment for me.

At school I participated in debates and took part in a couple of plays. Once I was in a recitation contest: "The Shooting of Dan McGrew" was my poem. My favorite subjects were mathematics and science. I took two years of Latin.

On the farm, one of the annual events was the hog-killing, usually on a cold December day. That was an exciting and busy time, with some of our neighbors participating. Before the day was over, the smokehouse was full of hams and shoulders. The women cooked the pork fat for lard and cracklings. Then, in the next few days, lots of sausages were stuffed and hung in the smokehouse.

In the summer time, after a good rain we could go swimming in a branch of the creek in our woodland. There was one special place where the water was then deep enough to dive into and swim.

I joined the Boy Scouts and became a First Class Scout. I also got several Merit badges, which included wood carving and bird-watching. I found that persimmon wood was very good for carving, and I made a wooden chain from a piece of persimmon.

The black tenant families on our farm had their own fields of tobacco, but all of us did some of the

Ralph's eighth-grade portrait, in 1924. He skipped the seventh grade.

For five years my husband Raymond (Ralph's brother) and I ran a store and service station at Hanrahan's Crossroads, on Highway 11. We lived in the back of the store.

The shooting happened in 1929, in the fall, during tobacco-curing time, when people were awake all night in their tobacco barns. Around 11 p.m. a car pulled up and its horn blew.

I told Ray to ignore it, but he went out, closing the door between our living quarters and the store. The next thing I heard was Ray calling, "Irma Belle, I've been shot!"

I knocked the door off its hinges and saw Ray outside, slumped against the screen door at the front of the store. I couldn't open the front door so I ran to the back of the store, pulled away the board that secured the back door, and ran out.

Two men were sitting in their car, watching me. A dog barked, and they drove off.

Ray had filled the gas tank and was adding oil when they shot him through the eyebrow, hoping to cripple him so they could rob the store. Ray staggered to the front door and fell against it so they couldn't get in.

I called the police and told them which direction the robbers had gone, and I called Dr. Randall Collins Smith, who came right out to take care of Raymond's wound. The police caught the men in the Kinston cemetery. They had broken out of jail in Rocky Mount.

The shooting at Raymond's store

As told by
Irma Belle Morris

work together, especially the harvesting. We always called the older blacks "Uncle" and "Aunt". For instance, one of the tenants was "Uncle Will." One of the tenants, a widow who had at one time been a school teacher, had a son named Ralph who was a little older than I.

My father and mother were strict parents, but they showed their love and concern in many ways. My father sometimes took me along when he was visiting neighbors. He taught me to drive a car when I was about 14. He was quite sentimental, and in times of sorrow he cried. This trait was fairly common in our family. It was very strong in my oldest brothers, and even in me.

The most remarkable thing about my father was his ability to calculate in his head. He could multiply fairly complicated figures almost instantly, without resort to paper and pencil. He was sometimes called upon to do the calculating at the tobacco market, but he did that only in an emergency.

The churches were very strong in our part of Pitt County. We went not only to the Ayden Christian Church but also to the special annual homecomings at Timothy, Roundtree, and other rural churches. Around 1920 there were a lot of revival meetings. Especially noteworthy were the meetings of "Cyclone Mack" McLendon.

Most of our travel was to visit relatives in Washington, Bath, New Bern, and other places in eastern North Carolina. The nearest beach was Atlantic Beach, across the bridge from Morehead City. At least once, I drove my father's car to Atlantic Beach and took some friends along.

Two of Ralph's Boy Scout badges.

Cultural events were not too frequent, but we attended certain things in Greenville. I remember the Chautauqua coming to Ayden, and minstrel shows and circuses. I believe I got as far as Richmond, in Virginia, and Wilmington and Raleigh, in North Carolina, during that time.

My oldest brother, Arthur, had married about 1920, and was not living with us on the farm. He had first worked in a bank in Vanceboro, and then for a furniture store in Ayden.

In 1923 my two oldest sisters, Estelle and Thelma, were married in a double wedding at our home. They married cousins, both Tuckers, and the occasion sticks in my memory.

The Ayden Rotary Club, founded in 1924, gave me a small scholarship, which helped me go to college. After I had won first place in the State math contest, my teachers and others urged me to go to the University of North Carolina at Chapel Hill. My father agreed to help pay my way.

That was my great step forward – a University education at one of the best universities of the South. I was truly faced with a great opportunity to learn, grow, and make my own way in the world.

AYDEN WINS FIRST PLACE STATE HIGH SCHOOL MATH TEST

Paper Submitted By Ralph Collins Awarded First Place Among Fifty - Six Contestants

Chapel Hill, June 7.—The Ayden high school, with the paper submitted by Ralph Collins, has won first place in the first annual high school mathematics contest for North Carolina high schools, it was announced today by E. R. Rankin, who has acted as secretary of the mathematics contest.

The Richard J. Reynolds high school, with the paper submitted by Sam Rose, was declared winner of second place in the contest.

The number of high schools which participated in the mathematics contest on May 6 was 56. In these 56 high schools, a total of 1,919 students stood the standard examination which had been prepared by the mathematics department of the University. Each high school submitted its best paper to the mathematics department of the University. From the mathematics department, a committee, consisting of Dr. Archibald Henderson, chairman, Dr. A. W. Hobbs, and Dr. J. W. Lasley, Jr., served as the examining committee and committee on award.

The mathematics contest was conducted under the joint auspices of the University Extension Division and the Department of Mathematics of the University of North Carolina. A trophy cup, signifying the State prize, will be awarded by the University Extension Division to the Ayden high school. The first annual mathematics contest, as guaged by the interest shown in it by the high schools and as guaged by the papers sent in to the University from the competing high schools, was regarded as very successful.

Ralph, left, with friends in 1927.

Venturing forth to college

At the University of North Carolina at Chapel Hill, I lived in Carr Dormitory the first year and after that in Grimes, Dormitory F, and one summer in Smith. I rented rooms in town, one year in the Hocutts' home, and one year while in Graduate School, at Mrs. Remsen's.

In Carr I was next to Bynum Gym, where all freshmen had compulsory PhysEd, calisthenics, and other forms of exercise. I always liked to exercise, and I later took up tennis as my main sport. I also took dance lessons from Estelle Lawson, the daughter of the gym director and later a noted tennis player.

I had no fixed idea about a subject to major in. I thought it might be Mathematics, and others seemed to expect that also. I took Differential and Integral Calculus, and Analytic Geometry. I found these courses very interesting, but in the meantime, I discovered other interests. I had had a general idea of trying to learn more of the basic sciences, so I started out with Botany, and then Physics, but I never got to Chemistry or Geology.

I had had some French in High School, so I continued it at Carolina. At the same time I started German. When I had had an equal amount of both, I felt that I could read French quite well, but German not as well. I therefore took more German and ended up with a major in German! That seems like a poor reason, but I think that I was also attracted by the mystic, philosophical quality of the German language and literature.

The campus in 1930. The Old Well stands in the center, in front of South Hall.

ORTH CAROLINA

Ralph, left, and friends. The men are dressed casually, in knickers.

At left: Carr Hall. Above: Bynum Gym; Grimes Dorm.

The University afforded many opportunities for cultural experiences. The Playmaker's Theater produced many plays, especially those of Paul Green, and other folk-play writers. The Music Department had many events. There were visiting attractions such as Ruth St. Denis and the Denishawn dance groups. The Kurt Joos Ballet performed *The Green Table*.

There were many speakers of national fame. Several times I heard Norman Thomas, the Socialist Party candidate for the US presidency between 1928 and 1948.

My most wonderful experience as a freshman was to find myself in an English class under one of the best professors in the Department, Howard Mumford Jones, who became reknowned as a writer and critic. Our main text was *A Modern Symposium*, a book of essays by G. Lowes Dickinson. We had to write a lot of papers, and I was doing fairly well, but not too sure of myself, in a class of obviously well-prepared students.

I got grades of B and perhaps a C on some of my papers. At the end of the course, we were asked to assume that we were part of the Symposium and to write our contribution. Evidently I gave it my best. Dr. Jones gave me an A on my paper, read parts of it before the class, and gave me an A in the course. I'll never forget the experience, and I adopted Dr. Jones' approach to grading when I became a College Professor.

At the same time, there was another surprise. I found myself a member of a discussion group led by Dean Addison Hibbard, Dean of the College of Liberal Arts. Evidently I was again among some of the best students. This time, however, I don't

Ralph in 1929, 1930, and 1931.

remember distinguishing myself in any way. Perhaps I was too shy, feeling that I was just a country boy, a bit out of his element.

During the first year I worked a few jobs in the kitchen at Swain Hall, the dining hall. I never waited on tables, but did dishwashing – with a machine.

I suppose I was something of a bookworm, but I did not, however, make a big thing out of exams. Whereas some of my friends would study way into the night for term exams, I would do my review of the course in the afternoon and then go to the movies the evening before the exam day. I felt that relaxation and a good night of sleep was better for me.

Furthermore, after my freshman year I began taking an extra course each quarter, so that at the end of three years, I lacked only a couple of courses for my degree. So I went to summer school in 1929 and finished my BA requirements. While I waited to get my degree in the spring of 1930 together with my class, I worked on my MA, which I got in 1931.

In addition to Howard Mumford Jones, some of my favorite professors were Dr. Coriden Lyons and Dr. Urban T. Holmes in French, Dr. James P. Harland in Archaeology, Dr. William M. Dey in French Romanticism, and Dr. Ernest L. Mackie and Dr. John W. Lasley in Mathematics.

In German I studied under Dr. Mentzenthin, Dr. Krumpelmann, Dr. Toy, and Dr. Kent Brown, in that order. Years later, after World War II, Dr. Krumpelmann and I worked together on a project in Germany. I studied Goethe with Prof. Toy, but did my Master's thesis, "Hebbel's Theory of Tragic Guilt," with Dr. Brown.

Swain Hall.

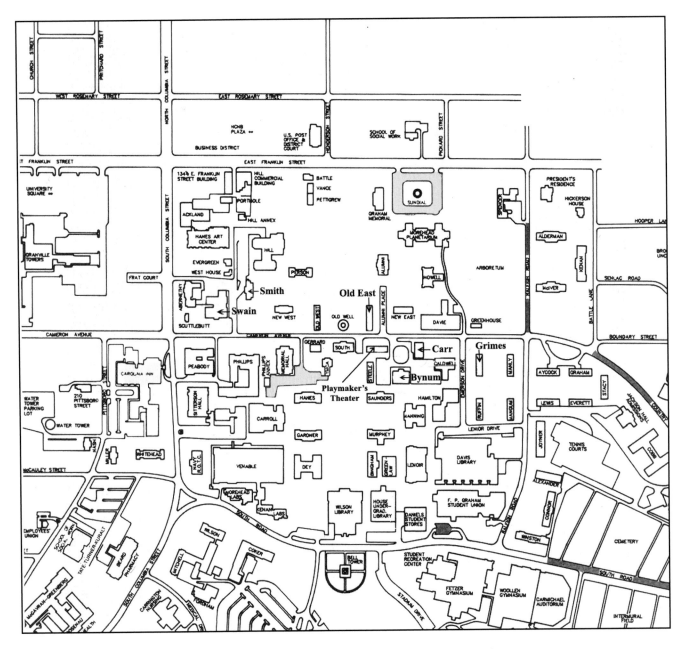

Arrows point to Swain Hall, Smith, Old East, Playmaker's Theater, Bynum, Carr, and Grimes.

Above: Playmaker's Theater. Below: the Old Well, left.

In 1926, when Dad went to UNC, the campus was quite small, and it was easy to walk from one side to the other.

Now the campus is huge, and with most visitor parking on the periphery, it's a challenging trek to reach the old campus. The Old Well is the landmark to look for when exploring the old campus.

Erica

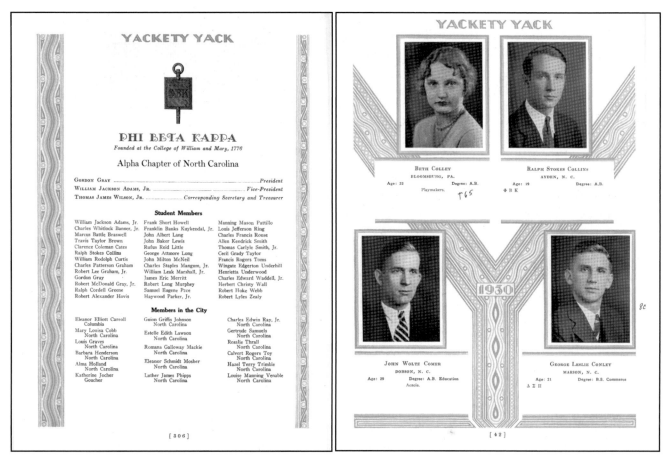

Ralph was inducted into Phi Beta Kappa in 1929.

Ralph graduated with his class in 1930.

Among my classmates at Carolina were Bill Speight and Willis Whichard, two men from Greenville, North Carolina. Among my closest friends were Clarence Coleman Cates, Ben Brodie, Fred Cole, John Lang, and Ralph Reid.

One classmate I do not recall from that time, Harold Urist, was head of the USIS unit in our Embassy in Montevideo in 1960-62, when I was First Secretary there. Another classmate whom I don't recall, Gordon Gray, became Secretary of War and later was President at UNC, in 1950-1955.

I had a teaching fellowship in German in 1929-30, while working on my MA. Early in 1930, Jim Bell, a German Instructor, committed suicide, under unexplained circumstance. I was then made Instructor in German, a position I held for the next two years.

My grade record was very good – I recall one B, on a course on the European Realistic Novel under Howard Mumford Jones. I wasn't really prepared for that course, but I wanted very much to take another course with him before he left for Michigan (and later Harvard). I have no regrets about that B; it was never my special goal to make a record of all A's.

The first two summers at UNC, 1927 and 1928, I spent on the farm near Ayden. In 1929 I stayed in Summer School. One summer Cecil "Pete" Taylor and I hitchhiked back from Ravenwood, West Virginia, through southern Ohio and the Cumberland Gap back to Eastern North Carolina.

Total:
30½ A's , 4 B's, 1½ C's
Total Average : 96.4233
Φ BK Average : 96.4166

Northern France from the port of Boulogne to Paris.

Europe
before the War

1932-1933

Rue de Rivoli in 1930, with the Tuileries Gardens on the right, and the Louvre in the distance.

Exploring Europe

It was probably a poor move on my part, because it was during the Depression of the 1930s, but in 1932 I decided to resign my job as Instructor in German at the University of North Carolina in order to study in Europe. Perhaps I could have had a leave of absence, but I did not ask for one.

Dr. Kent Brown had recommended that I study under Prof. Fritz Strich, in Munich. It turned out that Strich was no longer in Munich but in Zürich. This I did not find out until I had arrived in Munich, but I decided to stay in Munich anyway.

My good friend Pete Taylor wanted to spend the summer of 1932 in France, so we made our plans together. Pete went on to get his PhD in French at Chapel Hill and eventually joined the faculty of Louisiana State where he was Dean of Liberal Arts in the early 60's, then Chancellor of the Baton Rouge campus, and ultimately President of the University.

We sailed from New York on the *S.S. Rotterdam* and landed at Boulogne. We stayed a couple of weeks at a small hotel, the Delavigne, at 1 Rue Delavigne, near the Odéon Theater and next to the Luxembourg Gardens. We then started out on our Velo-moteurs, 1-horse-power mini-bikes, on a tour of France.

We went first to Fontainebleau, then to the Loire Valley chateaux and down to Tarbes, to visit a French family with whom Pete had corresponded. Then we went on to Lourdes, the Cirque de Gavarnie, Toulouse, Carcassonne, Nîmes, Marseille, Avignon, and then to Geneva.

Left: fishing on the banks of the Seine.
Above: Eiffel Tower, with bateau-mouche in foreground.
Top: L'Arc de Triomphe.

We really didn't have the proper papers to travel beyond Geneva in Switzerland, but we weren't fully aware of that, so we continued on to Interlaken and through the Furka and Grimsel Passes down to Luzerne. We were finally informed that we had no permit to be where we were; we took the shortest route to Basel and back into France.

Because we couldn't take our bikes into Germany without a fee, we left them in Strasbourg and took a train to Munich. Pete, whose main interest was France, wanted to spend only a short time in Germany. After Pete returned to Strasbourg, I bought a bicycle and went first to Salzburg, where I attended Mozart's *Così fan tutte* at the Festival and the Max Rheinhard staging of *Jedermann* (Everyman) in the cathedral square.

Back to Munich I went, and off on a bicycle tour of Germany of about 3,000 miles. I first went to Nürnberg. That part of my tour taught me an important lesson; to follow valleys in planning a trip by bicycle. The ridges I had to cross between Munich and Nürnberg were really exhausting, and I repeatedly had to push my bicycle uphill.

In general I stayed at Youth Hostels (Jugendherbergen). I still have my membership card, dated June 30, 1932. The card cost me five marks, and each overnight in a hostel cost about 30 cents. I stayed at Würzburg, Frankfurt-am-Main, Mainz, Koblenz, Bonn, Münster, Hildesheim, Braunschweig, Jena, Leipzig, Stralsund, Rostock, Bremen, Aachen, Trier, Karlsruhe, Freiburg and Ulm, the last on October 7.

I did not always stay at Youth Hostels. In cities where I wanted to go to the theater or opera, I stayed at small hotels, because in the Hostels you had to be

Clockwise from top left:
Breslau; Beaugency;
Marienplatz and City Hall,
Munich; old house in
Tours; Heidelberg Castle;
Cologne Cathedral
Center: Velo-moteurs.

in bed by 10 p.m. The facilities in the Hostels were good and clean.

During the summer months they were quite full; as fall arrived, some were almost empty. I remember that in Prum I was alone, and the family that ran the Hostel invited me into their warm kitchen. They said they were delighted to have an American in their house because they had had American soldiers in their home at the end of World War I and liked Americans very much.

On this trip I took the Rhine boat trip from Mainz to Koblenz, and all of us sang Heine's "Lorelei" as we passed the Lorelei rock. I visited Beethoven's home in Bonn, and Eisenach, where Johann Sebastian Bach was born, and Wartburg castle.

In Weimar I stayed in a Pension that had been the home of Frau von Stein, Goethe's friend. It was extremely pleasant. I shall always remember how the bees were plentiful around the honey pots, and how we sometimes imprisoned them for a while under overturned water glasses.

In Weimar I also met a couple from Oberlin College, the Harrouns. He was head of the music department, and she taught German. I will always remember the pleasant time we had, including an evening performance of Mozart's "Eine kleine Nachtmusik." In Dresden I did not stay at a hostel, but I spent a couple of days enjoying the Zwinger, a magnificent Baroque palace, and Dresden's art galleries.

A few times, instead of riding my bicycle, I put it on the baggage car of a train and rode to the next city, retrieving my bicycle on arrival. This brought about an unusual situation in Breslau. I arrived by

View of the Rhine. The Lorelei Rock is on the right bank, where the river makes a sharp turn.

50

train about 9 p.m. and asked at the information desk about lodging. I was directed to a place across the square that turned out to be run by nuns. I assume they usually helped female travelers – but lo and behold – they took me in for the night. I felt rather embarrassed by this situation.

Going from Breslau to Berlin, I encountered another unusual situation. The distance was a little over 180 miles. When I arrived in Frankfurt-an-der-Oder, it was mid-afternoon, so I thought I would go a bit farther before stopping for the night. It was far from my thought to ride all the way to Berlin that day. However, as I got closer to Berlin and started inquiring about lodging, I was repeatedly told that there was none until I got to Berlin.

When I reached the outskirts of Berlin, I was told I could get lodging only in the center of Berlin – at least 20 miles away. By now it was dark. I had no lamp on my bicycle, so when I met a policeman, he said I would have to walk and push. When I left the policeman behind, I mounted my bike and pedaled on until I was stopped again.

Finally I arrived at a lodging, described by a policeman as being for Boy Scouts, which turned out to be an expensive hotel. I spent the night there, but moved to less expensive quarters the following day. I spent several days in Berlin, attending plays and operas and sightseeing.

I also spent a few days in Hamburg. The rest of my trip: over to the edge of Belgium and back down the Rhine to Freiburg and then back to Munich for Oktoberfest, only to find that Oktoberfest is mainly in September and was already over!

Kaiserstuben in Hotel Deutscher Kaiser, Munich.

Frau Kloeck, on her apartment balcony.

Attending the University of Munich

In Munich I lived with a German family, the Kloecks, in a fifth-floor apartment at 30 Jägerstrasse. It was near the Odeonsplatz, just off Ludwigstrasse, and only a few blocks from the University of Munich. Herr Kloeck was a druggist at the Storchenapotheke, just off Marienplatz.

Herr and Frau Kloeck had a daughter "Motti" who was engaged to an engineering student at the Technische Hochschule, Werner Hucke from Santiago, Chile, where his family had a confectionery enterprise. Later someone told me that "Hucke's Cookies" was a well-known brand in Chile.

The family was very nice to me, and I'll never forget how on Christmas Eve, when I had thought of going to the theater, they insisted that I have dinner and spend the evening with them, because they thought anyone unfortunate who could not spend that evening in a family group. Later on an Italian student, Bruno Arzeni, also came to live in the apartment. He was a very fine person, and I understand that he was later a German Professor at the University of Rome.

I had three main professors at the University. Under Walther Rehm, I studied 19th Century German Drama, Lessing, the Storm and Stress Period *(Sturm und Drang)*, the Impressionistic Novel, and Naturalism and Impressionism. Under Wilhelm Barcherdt, I studied German Classical Period, German Romanticism, and the History of German Lyric Poetry. Under Arthur Kutscher, I studied German Theater in the 18th and 19th Centuries.

Ralph's student ID card at the University of Munich.

I also sat in on other courses that my friends told me about. The one I remember best was on German Opera, and the professor, in spite of his advanced years, sang beautifully to illustrate the music of various German operas.

Munich was a great place for opera. I went regularly, paying very little for student seats in the back of the theater. During the winter season they did all the Wagnerian operas from *Rienzi* to *Parsifal*. At the time I was quite taken with Wagner; it was only several years later that I lost my enthrallment and learned to be critical of their length and slowness of action. My favorite example was the peremptory demand that the lady go immediately, and a half-hour later she was still there singing away.

I got to see and hear all the Mozart operas, in a jewel of a theater called the Residenztheater, next to the Nationaltheater, and I heard unusual operas, such as Pfitzner's *Palestrina*. I also went to a lot of plays.

Munich was a delightful city to live in. The main feature of the winter season was the celebration of Fasching, the pre-Lenten carnival season leading up to Mardi Gras. During Fasching costume balls were everywhere, as many as 15-20 every night. My friends and I went to quite a few.

The most elaborate and and for me the most memorable was the Foreign Students Ball at the Hotel Vier Jahreszeiten (Four Seasons). It had eight different types of orchestras in eight ballrooms, all full of people. We wandered from one ballroom to the next. At midnight we tried to make it down into one of the bars to drink champagne. Some Fasching balls seemed to go on all night long. We stayed late, but not to the very end.

Herr Kloeck.

Adolph Hitler.

Hitler's Munich headquarters.

Nazi book burnings, part of the alignment of the arts with Nazi Party goals, began in May 1930 in a nationwide "cleansing by fire." Students in university towns burned books denounced as un-German.

Banned, along with all Jewish books, were leading German writers, such as Bertold Brecht, and foreign authors, including Ermest Hemingway and Helen Keller. New books had to conform to Nazi views and had to stress topics such as the camaraderie of war and Nazi views on race.

In a fairly short time I found myself part of a small group of students who met frequently and did a lot of things together. It was rather international: three or four Germans, a man (Hermann Tersteeg) from Leyden, Holland, a couple from South Africa, a musician (Walter Ducloux) from Switzerland, and two other Americans.

We spoke only German. I didn't ever say anything in English to my fellow Americans. As a matter of fact, I didn't speak English for more than six months. I was in "total immersion" in Germany.

Among the things we did together was to go on the Theater History excursions sponsored by Professor Kutscher. We went to such theaters as a Bauerntheater (peasant theater) in the village of Siegsdorf, to a local theater in Partenkirchen, and to the theater in Augsburg. While at Partenkirchen, we also went skiing in the mountains at Garmisch.

Thomas Mann, Ralph's favorite German author.

The political situation in Germany at this time was chaotic. The NSDAP (Deutsche Arbeiter Partei), or Nazi Party, with Adolf Hitler at the head, kept things in an uproar. The Brown House, Hitler's Munich headquarters, was only a few blocks from where I lived. I frequently saw him on his balcony. The Party was also active in the University.

One evening there was a book-burning. Some of my friends and I started out to see what was going on, but the whole idea became so repugnant that we went elsewhere.

At spring vacation, I took advantage of the fact that train fare to Rome had been reduced for a Fascist anniversary. Dietrich Stern, a friend from Breslau, decided to go with me. Bruno Arzeni arranged for us to stay in his aunt's apartment in Rome, on Via

Mussolini addressing the crowd from his balcony on the Piazza Venezia.

Babbuino. The evening before our departure, we heard Hitler make his last pre-election speech. We stopped in Bologna and Florence on the way to Rome.

While in Rome we saw Mussolini on his balcony – Piazza Venezia – and we made a trip down to Naples and Capri. In the meantime Hitler's move against Jews took an ugly turn, and Dietrich's father, who was Supreme Court Justice for Silesia, was removed from office because he was one-eighth Jewish. Dietrich was afraid to return to Germany so I returned without him.

At Pentecost, an important holiday in South Germany, I had planned to take a trip to Budapest via Vienna. An attack of appendicitis and an operation prevented this. I went to a private clinic near where I lived. On the fourth or fifth day, the doctor sent me home. I told him that I lived on the fifth floor. He said, "Good! Be sure to go for a walk every day!"

If I had been in America, I would probably have been kept in the hospital for more than two weeks. Since then doctors have learned to get people up early after an operation. My surgeon in Munich was ahead of us.

I did no other special travel in Europe. In August I returned to Paris, and after a week there I sailed from Boulogne on the new *S.S. Statendam*, back to New York.

Piazza di Spagna, Rome.

Guidebook cover.

Maryville, Tennessee, with Elm Avenue at upper center left.

USA

1933-1945

Returning to North Carolina

When I arrived in New York, I had enough money to take a bus to North Carolina, but not enough to take the train! I arrived at home with very little money in my pocket – but, just imagine! – I had spent 14 months in Europe, had paid my passage there and back, and had spent only about $1,100. With our inflation since then it is hard to believe it was possible.

By this time my father and mother and their two youngest daughters were no longer living on the farm, but had moved to Ayden. I was without a job, so I helped a bit on grading tobacco.

Then I got a job with the Mason County Agriculture Administration, measuring tobacco fields to see that the acreage planted was in accordance with the allotments under the AAA (the Agricultural Adjustments Administration, in the US Department of Agriculture), which was part of Franklin D. Roosevelt's New Deal.

That at least gave me a little income. In the severe Depression at that time, it helped me a lot.

The sudden death of our mother, on June 2, 1934, was a tremendous loss to the whole family. While she was attending a program at the College in Greenville, she had a heart attack. By the time she was taken to my sister Estelle's house, Mother was dead. I was not present – for some reason I had not gone to Greenville.

Were the chickens responsible for Margaret Collins' death? Margaret had a flock of 50 chickens. At night she ran them into the chicken house so the rats wouldn't get them.

She also did it before leaving Ayden to go to Greenville for her daughter Rosa's graduation ceremonies, in 1934.

Margaret got overheated and was out of breath when she got into the car. Rosa drove, and when they arrived at the college, Margaret fell over before she could get out of the car.

Rosa drove to her sister Estelle's house, where they called the doctor and then took Margaret to the hospital. She died en route, having suffered a heart attack at age 57.

Irma Belle Morris

The Collins house in Ayden in 1938.

The Stokes house, where Margaret lived as a girl.

During the Depression, Uncle Ralph and I sold records for 35¢ a piece at a Record Bar in my father's furniture store in Greenville. We would play a line or two of a record for the customer to let him hear what the piece was like, but we never played the whole piece. The record players at that time were hand-cranked Victrolas.

John Arthur Collins II

In the 1930s Ralph and his brother Raymond, my father, worked for Mason County Agriculture Administration, measuring tobacco land.

The value of a farm was equal to the number of acres that could be planted in tobacco.

Each farm was given an allotment that could be planted in tobacco and the Collins brothers were responsible for land measurement.

Raymond L. Collins, Jr.

The Agricultural Adjustment Act of 1933 was created to help farmers by reducing the production of staple crops, thus raising farm prices and encouraging more diversified farming. Farmers received payments in return for limiting acreage for staple crops; in the case of cotton and tobacco, coercive taxes forced farmers to cut the amounts they sold.

Ralph's brother Raymond posed in a tobacco field about 1950 for this picture, used in an advertisement for Smith's-Douglas Fertilizer.

After a period of mourning, that left my father and youngest sister, Margaret, alone in the house in Ayden. Margaret, who had never been a very healthy child, died a few years later, on June 27, 1939, at age 21. Soon thereafter my father moved to Greenville and lived with my older brother, Jim Ed.

Although I had taught three years at the University level, I could not teach at all in North Carolina high schools because I had not taken the Education courses required for a Teacher's Certificate.

In order to remedy this situation, I enrolled for the winter and spring terms of 1934 at East Carolina Teacher's College in Greenville. While I worked on my teaching degree there, I lived with my oldest brother, John Arthur, and his family.

With the proper credits, I got a Certificate and then got a job to teach French at the Charles L. Coon High School in Wilson, North Carolina. During the 1934-35 school year, I lived in a private home there.

Ralph's future bride, Maria Johanna Zubiller, at age 16, in 1932.

Embarking on a college teaching career

In the meantime, two other things happened. I was asked to teach German in the University of North Carolina Summer School in 1935. Next a friend, Dr. Hill Shine, whom I had met in the early 1930s at Chapel Hill and who was teaching English at Maryville College in Tennessee, recommended me for a job in the Foreign Language Department there.

I came to Maryville for an interview with Dr. Lloyd, Dean Hunter, and Dr. Wayne Davis, head of the Foreign Language Department. I was hired to teach French and German and came to Maryville, beginning the fall term of 1935. I lived at the home of Professor Davis on Miller Street the next two years.

I began thinking about more graduate work in order to get my PhD. I considered Northwestern and Wisconsin, which had strong German Departments, but finally decided on Johns Hopkins.

Dr. Ernst Feise at Johns Hopkins was also the Director of the Middlebury College German Summer School. There were other strong German professors on the Summer School faculty: Dr. Hohlfeld of Wisconsin and Dr. Gaede of Queens College.

By studying two summers at the Middlebury College Summer School, I was able to get enough credits, along with my credits from the University of Munich, to make it possible for me to finish my PhD requirements at Johns Hopkins in one year. I wrote my dissertation on "The Artist in Modern German Drama" and received my PhD in June 1938.

Ralph and Maria met when they attended the German summer school at Middlebury College, Vermont.

Clockwise from top left: German folk dancing on the campus; cooking out, hiking, and relaxing in the mountains;

Prof. Ernst Feise, director of the school and Ralph's professor at Johns Hopkins.

Clockwise from top left:

Maria in Vermont in 1937;

Ralph in June 1938, when he received his PhD in German Language and Literature from Johns Hopkins;

at Johns Hopkins in 1937-1938.

Maria and Ralph with her parents, Maria and Alfred Zubiller, in front of the Old Cadet Chapel, at West Point.

The Middlebury College Summer School was an important key in my life in another special way. It was there that I met Maria Johanna Zubiller from West Point, New York, and we were married on August 17, 1938.

When I returned to Maryville College in September 1938, my colleagues and friends at Maryville were more surprised by my marriage than they were impressed by my degree. Certainly the two together were crowning moments in my life — and my friends were quite right in considering the acquisition of a wonderful wife as by far the more important.

Maria and I were married in the old Cadet Chapel in West Point, NY and Ralph Colbert of the Music faculty at Maryville College was Best Man. My oldest brother, Arthur, came up from North Carolina with his wife Lula Mae and son John, Jr. A wedding banquet was held at Storm King Arms in Cornwall-on-Hudson, New York.

After the wedding we went to New York City, then to Washington, DC, to Natural Bridge, Virginia, and on to Maryville. After a few days in Maryville we went to Greenville, Eastern North Carolina, to buy furniture from the store owned by my brother John Arthur. With the help of my brother Raymond, we returned home with the furniture, crossing the Smoky Mountains at Newfound Gap.

We had very little money, so we did not have a car the first two years. We traveled everywhere by train or bus. We lived at first in one of Mrs. King's apartments on High Street. For a short time our good friends Andy and Flo Alexander lived downstairs.

Natural Bridge, Virginia, as it looked in 1938 when Ralph and Maria visited it on their honeymoon. This picture always hung on the wall in their home.

In North Carolina in 1938.

Christmas in Maryville in 1939.

Sunday at Clingman's Dome.

Lunch break during hike up Cove Mountain in the Smokies in 1939.

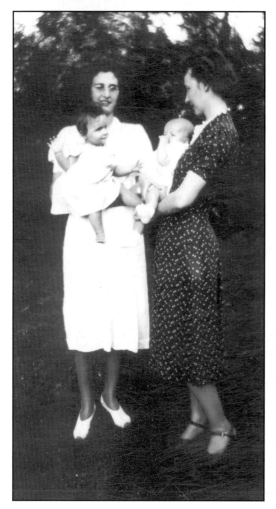

Clockwise from bottom left: Maria holds Erica and Flo Alexander holds her son Lamar, in September 1940;

the house on Elm Avenue (now Clarion Avenue);

at Newfound Gap in the Smokies in January 1941;

Maria Zubiller meets her new grandson, Randall, in August 1941;

Ralph and Erica at Maryville graduation in June 1941;

an outing in September 1941.

Left: Meeting a black bear in the Smoky Mountains National Park.

Above (left to right): Verton Queener, Ralph, Andy Alexander, and Lyn Queener.

Randall learning to walk at the Zubiller home in Cornwall-on-Hudson.

Clockwise from far right: Ralph and Erica in 1942; at Laurel Falls in the Smoky Mountains in 1943; Erica and Randall, Easter 1943; at Maryville graduation in 1942.

In Tennessee in January 1944.

Our first child, Erica, was born on January 3, 1940, and Lamar Alexander was born six months later. Erica was born in the Fort Craig Hospital early in the morning, so I was late for Chapel at the College on that day.

We were very proud of our first-born, who was soon followed by our son, Randall, on July 29, 1941, and our daughter Mary Johanna, on November 18, 1943. I took pleasure in wheeling Erica around the neighborhood. In order to have more room, we moved into a house on Elm Avenue. Many a time I sat in my armchair with two kids on my lap and read them stories. All three learned to read a bit before they went to grade school, and all three attended Flo Alexander's nursery school.

At the College I was very busy, now teaching mostly German. I had an article published in the February 1942 issue of *Germanic Review*, entitled "Hermann Bahr's Die Mutter."

I joined the South Atlantic Modern Language Association, and the Tennessee Philological Society, and I attended most of their meetings. I read my paper on Hermann Bahr at a meeting of the Modern Language Association in New York. [At that time the MLA was a discussion and advocacy group for the study of literature and modern languages.]

Locally, Maria helped me with a German Club, and her father helped entertain the students. I guess that German folk-dancing was the first kind of dancing permitted at Maryville College.

Randall and Erica with Mary Johanna in January 1944.

Joining the war effort in World War II

When the War started, I tried to get into the Naval Reserve, but I was turned down, first as underweight, and then for poor eyesight.

The full realization of Maryville's involvement in the War came with the arrival on campus of the first unit of Army Air Force Training Corps in May 1942. Maryville was one of 151 colleges that contracted to furnish 300 cadets each with quarters, meals, medical care, and instruction in Math, Physics, English, Geography, History, Civil Air Regulations, and Physical Training.

The cadets entered enthusiastically into the social life of the campus. Rules for women were relaxed somewhat. Dating was allowed daily from breakfast to evening study hours, for designated evening functions, and at Sunday services.

Dating on Sunday afternoons and study nights was still prohibited. These regulations applied to all students, including cadets. The no-dancing rule was still in effect, and the no-smoking rule for students.

Women were allowed to go home to see fiancés or relatives home on furlough. Permissions to marry were more frequent, as men going overseas wanted to marry before they left. Those who married without permission were, as before, suspended. A modicum of equality was introduced in April 1943, when rules required men to be in their rooms by 11 p.m. Violations occurred frequently.

Dearest Maria,

Washington DC
March 9, 1945

. . . .This morning I went to get some passport photographs taken. Then I went to the Naval Dispensary, had a tetanus shot and a blood-type test, and got a schedule for further shots: yellow fever, cowpox, second tetanus, typhus. Cholera and bubonic plague inoculations depend upon what foreign assignment I get.

. . . .Some of the girls for whom I filled out papers yesterday asked whether my family was going with me to my post. So just get yourself set for a trip abroad before this year is out. Maybe you and the children will have to take some of those nice shots. . . .

Washington DC
March 10, 1945

. . . .A Mr. Cummings, at the Division of Foreign Activity Correlation. . . wants me to work under him with a group in London, France, and Germany on a matter of strategic documents. He says it is a very important assignment, and wants to send me over as soon as possible. . . . He said that I might be sent out as soon after March 20 as transportation can be arranged.

. . . . If I go by plane, I shall be permitted to take only 55 or 65 pounds. That leaves the trunk out. Some officers have the Army-officers-type duffel bag. I priced one here today at $29.50. That's outrageous for a canvas bag and I shall not get one. . . .

It's quite a shock to think I may go so soon. I certainly would like to see you and the children before I have to leave.

Washington DC
March 13, 1945

Yesterday and today I have spent in finding out more about my assignment. Almost everything connected with it is very secret, but maybe I can say more about it when the fighting stops. . . .

Washington DC
March 20, 1945

. . . .This is the official language of the basic part of my new appointment: "You are now appointed Vice Consul at London, England, for duty on the Staff of the Honorable Robert D. Murphy, United States Political Advisor on German Affairs,

Supreme Headquarters, Allied Expeditionary Forces, and you should plan to proceed to your post as soon as possible."

. . . .I have just learned that I am to leave by boat Wed. from N.Y. It is awful hard to leave you behind, but I hope that you will get along all right, and that we may meet in good health and in peace in London in July. . . .Good-bye, darling, and good-bye, Erica, Randall, and Mary Johanna. We shall meet again soon.

Washington DC
March 26, 1945

. . . .It's probably a good thing that I did come. Father [Alfred Zubiller] was very much opposed to your going to London with the children. After he had made many objections, I finally said that we would get to come home every two years for a two-month visit. Well, that made things different – and he thought it would be all right. So now, you won't have any opposition from that quarter. . . .

Cornwall-on-Hudson, NY
March 29, 1945

. . . .I shall write you tomorrow, so I shall not close this letter with good-bye. Write me all about the children and the events of Maryville.

. . . .I got back from Cornwall last night before nine o'clock and have bought some books to take along on board ship:

Nevins & Commager, "Short History of U.S."	$.95
Hansen, "America's Role in the World Economy"	2.50
Stettinius, "Lend Lease"	.25
"The Next Germany"	.25
Temple, "Christianity and the Social Order"	.25

New York City
March 30, 1945

. . . .Several hours from now I shall be on board ship. It would have been so much fun to have you and the children along. I shall think of you constantly until I shall see you again. Good-bye, darling, and I love you more than I can tell. Good-bye Erica, Randall, and Mary. Daddy will be thinking of you.

Love and kisses, Ralph

The State Department when Ralph Collins joined it

Before World War II, the State Department was one of the smallest departments of the US government. Traditionally, Ambassadors and Consuls were political appointments made by the President.

In 1924 a Foreign Service was set up, which staffed 15 embassies abroad, along with 65 consulates general and 180 consulates.

Embassies existed only in large, important countries. A Consul General was a kind of mini-ambassador in less important places, and a Consul (the post Ralph held in Bilbao) chiefly issued visas to foreigners desiring to travel to the US and looked after US citizens and interests in the region where the Consulate was located.

Foreign Service Officers were permanent employees who did not leave office when a new political administration won the Presidency.

World War II brought a huge expansion of US involvement abroad, not just in the war zones, but also in dealings with allied countries and with countries that might go either way in the struggle.

In Washington, many new agencies were created – Foreign Economic Assistance, War Production Administration, Office of Lend Lease Administration, Office of War Information – and they also sent personnel abroad. Some of these agencies were nominally coordinated with the State Department, but relationships were casual and sometimes chaotic.

Ralph Collins was recruited by the State Department with the rank of Vice Consul (a traditional position, usually concerned with issuing visas). Instead he ended up working with a British Colonel from the British Foreign Office, after which he was assigned for a while to an Army Intelligence unit where he checked out military information.

At the end of the war, the so-called Auxiliary Officers who had been brought in during the war were allowed to take examinations to become regular Foreign Service Officers. After some bureaucratic snafus, Ralph made the transition from an auxiliary to a regular officer in June 1946.

By the time Ralph arrived at the US Embassy in Moscow, in 1949, the State Department had taken on a much more complex organizational structure.

The Embassy had several sections: a Political Section, headed by the Political Officer, who usually had the rank of First Secretary; an Economic Section; an Agricultural Section; an Information Officer; a Consular Section; and a Military Attaché, who was an officer in the Army or Navy.

Moreover, back in Washington, the State Department was organized into geographical areas, for European Affairs, Far Eastern Affairs, Middle Eastern and African Affairs, and Latin-American Affairs.

When I was a teenager, I asked Dad what he did all day at his office. He replied rather casually, "Shuffling papers."

Then he explained in more detail that as Political Officer he had to make reports on what was happening in the local political situation; these had to be made into multiple copies (in those days, carbon paper and typewriters were used, as copying machines did not yet exist, much less desktop computers).

Copies were sent to all the embassy sections that might need the information, and also to Washington, to the Department's geographical offices and the Political Section and other specialists.

In the field of organizational sociology, by the way, the problem of how to divide up an organization, by geography or by functional specialties, is considered an insoluble dilemma.

On a personal level, the friends that Ralph mentions socializing with are generally these various specialized officers at the US embassy and in some instances the officers at British and other embassies.

Randall Collins

S.S. Maryville Victory. Its keel was laid December 28, 1944, and it was launched February 22, 1945. Named for US colleges and universities, Victory ships were made for the US Maritime Commission in 1944-1945 expressly to haul cargo across the Atlantic after the War. The builder of *S.S. Maryville Victory*, California Shipbuilding, was the second-largest emergency shipyard in the US, delivering on average 1 ship every 72 hours starting September, 1941, including 306 Liberty ships, 30 tankers, 30 attack transports, and 51 Victory ships.

I did find ways to make a contribution to the War effort. I taught Math to the cadets. In the summer of 1943 I worked in the personnel office of Stone and Webster, builders of Y-12 (hutments, or prefabricated portable housing units for the military). The following summer I worked for ALCOA, nearby, in John Kenst's office of tests and measurements.

On my return from Europe in the fall of 1933, when I was without a job, I had written to the Department of State in Washington asking about entry into the American Foreign Service. The reply was that they had no entrance examinations scheduled and did not know when any would be held.

At Christmas 1944, I was in Washington to attend an MLA meeting with another faculty member, Dr. Verton Queener. I happened to hear that the Department of State was setting up a special group to go into Germany at the end of the War to seek out personnel and documents relating to the War's start.

I went down to the Department and talked to Walton Ferris, who was heading up the project. I was offered a job. After security clearance – the FBI questioned my friends – I was hired.

I spent about a month in Washington and then was given a date to sail to England in early April 1945. My wife took over two of my German courses at the College, and I departed for London, arriving the day that President Roosevelt died.

I was launched on a very different career. It was one that I and my family enjoyed very much.

Diagram of Berlin air lift.

Europe
after the War

1945-1948

Assignment: London

I traveled from New York to Southampton on the *S.S. Sea Wolf*, a converted Victory vessel that was bringing wounded soldiers back to the United States. Many of the passengers were in large rooms with several other people. I shared a stateroom with a gentleman who was the Canadian representative of William Grant and Sons. We had a very pleasant time together. Our ship was in convoy – I suppose one of the last convoys of World War II.

Arriving late in the afternoon at Southampton, we took a train to London. There we were housed in a small hotel on Cromwell Road.

When we asked where we could get supper, the landlady said that all the Americans ate at Grosvenor House. She meant, we learned the next day, that they all ate at the big cafeteria set up especially for the American troops and others in the basement of Grosvenor House.

When we arrived there, the cafeteria had long since closed for the evening, and we found ourselves in the awkward position of getting something to eat in mid-evening in one of the most luxurious – and expensive – hotels in London.

My fellow diners included people with UNRRA (United Nations Refugee Relief Association). That was to my advantage a couple of days later as a black tie was part of their uniform and I was able to borrow one to attend the service at St. Paul's

St. Paul's Cathedral had been a prime target during the Nazi Blitz. Above is one of the volunteers who kept a constant lookout for Nazi bombers and rockets. Other volunteers made up a bucket brigade.

Cathedral in memory of President Roosevelt. Winston Churchill was in attendance also.

On arrival in London I was issued an officer's uniform and all the stuff going with it – duffel bag and so on. We were considered officer rank (Captain), but we were supposed to wear an arm patch identifying us as US civilians. The military uniform protected us under the terms of the Geneva Convention, in case we were apprehended by the enemy; anyone not in uniform was treated as a spy. We wore these uniforms the first year or so but gradually abandoned them for civilian clothes.

Every weekday for a couple of weeks I met with other members of my group at the Foreign Office – it was a joint American-British operation. Among my group were Gardener Carpenter and Ted Reynolds. My official title was Vice Consul, Office of the US Political Adviser, Supreme Headquarters, Allied Expeditionary Forces, Europe. That was shortened to POLAD, SHAEF.

It was my first visit to London, and because our daily meetings at the Foreign Office were only in the morning, I had an opportunity to do a lot of sightseeing for about two weeks.

I had just arranged for tickets for Stratford when we were transferred to France. We were housed near Paris, in quarters called Père Vatel, in Versailles. It was cold, and I'll never forget sitting in the Paris Opera (Gounod's *Faust*) in my army overcoat. There was no heat.

Grosvenor House, London, in 2005.

Dearest Maria,

London

April 15, 1945

. . . .Yesterday afternoon I had a long walk thru downtown. There was much damage in places, but the general appearance is pretty good.

. . . .I am able to get my meals at the American Officer's Mess. It is dirt cheap and the best food in the city. Dinner is $.30 and sometimes $.25; breakfast $.20. Meals in the city run about $1.00.

. . . .It was an awful shock to get the news of President Roosevelt's death right after getting here. It caused quite a stir. I have a ticket to a special memorial service tomorrow. . . .

London

April 19, 1945

. . . .Yesterday I had a lot of hard work in purchasing my army outfit. . . .I was allowed $130 to buy the things. . . .When I leave here I shall leave all my civilian clothes here at the Embassy. My "assimilated rank" is that of 2nd Lt., but I shall wear no insignia of rank, and I shall neither give nor receive salutes.

I am planning to go up to Stratford next week for the Shakespeare festival. I shall see either "Much Ado" or "Twelfth Night." I am excited, of course.

London

April 21, 1945

It seems that we shall be leaving here very shortly. . . .My travel orders now permit me to take my family to Versailles. However, it is not yet actually possible for you to go there.

. . . .I think it would be best for you to sit tight and wait long enough to see how far you are permitted to go. You could stay on in Maryville or store the furniture and go on up to Cornwall. It doesn't seem advisable to go to all the trouble of moving to London for such a short time.

. . . .There hasn't been any mail yet. . . .The slowness of communication will make it hard to get together on the time for you to come over. Perhaps when I know definitely I can send you a cable.

. . .We arrived here yesterday and are fairly comfortably installed. It is an old hotel which is used for army billets. Three of us are in one large room with one regular bed and two steel cots. We have mattresses and blankets, no sheets or pillows. Next to the room is a good-sized bathroom. There is hot water. It gave me a queer feeling to find on a closet shelf a bottle of stuff for athlete's foot left there by a German soldier. So this was previously a billet for German soldiers.

We get our meals at an officer's mess for $1.00 per day. The dining room is in one of the Queen's palaces. Some of our offices are in the same building. . . .

Versailles
April 25, 1945

. . . .We Americans are at a very great disadvantage in the civilian economy. The official rate of exchange is 1 franc = 2 cents, but the actual black market rate is 1 franc = 1/2 cent.

. . . .Considering the present disadvantage of the exchange, it would be a little difficult to live here on a civilian basis. However, I expect that eventually we may find our work concentrated for a while at some smaller place in Germany, where living conditions will be fairly reasonable.

Let us hope that it will turn out that way. I have definite information that makes me hope for such a development, but I can't disclose it at the present. In the meantime, stay where you are until I let you know.

Versailles
April 30, 1945

. . . .I now have orders to go forward. I shall be away from here about a month. That is, unless I get orders in the meantime to go elsewhere. I have not had any mail from you yet. . . . I shall have a new APO number, but I don't think it would do any good for you to use it. . . .this will be my place of reference. . . .It is still morning here and it is barely possible that I may get something from you today in the two mails.. . . .I was lucky this morning to get a French woman to launder three shorts and a pair of pyjamas for me before I have to leave. . . .I miss you, darling, and I hope that we shall not be separated too much longer.

Versailles
May 7, 1945

Love, Ralph

The US 3rd Armored Division entered the newly captured German town of Marburg on March 28, 1945. The road is lined by liberated Polish citizens whom the Nazis had conscripted to do labor.

Assignment: Germany

We had a rather haphazard way of getting into Germany. It was arranged that we could serve in US Army Intelligence. I was given orders taking me to Wiesbaden, and my transportation was a weapons-carrier. The driver and I were the sole occupants.

We spent the night at a military camp near Luxembourg and witnessed the fireworks celebrating the end of the War that very day. The next day I was delivered to Wiesbaden, where I was assigned a room at the Hotel Schwarzer Bock, in peacetime one of the most fashionable hotels in town.

My first assignment in Germany was to a 7th Army Intelligence camp near Kassel, called Camp Dentine. I was assigned a jeep and a chauffeur and was given intelligence targets to check out. Actually I was then doing work for the military.

It was an interesting experience which took me into some unusual places. For example, to investigate the Library of the University of Göttingen, we had to go into the salt mine where the Library had been moved for safekeeping during the war.

The condition of German cities was horrible. Some of them were completely flattened by the bombing. When driving through Kassel, for instance, we had to pay strict attention to the military direction signs because there were no distinctive landmarks, only rubble.

Allies take over Berlin in 1945: Gen. Sokolowsky, Russia; Amb. Murphy, USA; Field Marshal Montgomery, Great Britain; Marshal Zhukov, Russia; Gen. Eisenhower, USA; Gen. Koenig, France; and Amb. Seminov, Russia.

Special efforts will be made to preserve from destruction all records, books, documents, papers, files, scientific, industrial and other information and data belonging to or controlled by the following:

a. The German Reich or any agency of government in Germany, whether central, regional, or local;
b. German military and para-military organizations; agencies and societies engaged in military research or propaganda;
c. All police organizations, including security and political police;
d. The Nazi Party and its affiliates;
e. Nazi economic organizations and industrial establishments;
f. Institutes and special bureaus devoting themselves to race, political, or similiar research. . . . .

Robert Murphy, January 1945

Ralph (left) and fellow officer.

Berlin lay in ruins. Above: Soviet army truck. Below: the Reichstag (left) and the Brandenburg Gate.

TOP SECRET.

Discovery of Secret Archives of German Foreign Ministry.

On May 12 I was in Muehlhausen (Thuringia) for the purpose of examining certain Foreign Ministry archives. By a fortunate coincidence I ran into Dr. Ralph Collins, of the State Department, a member of the U. S. Team working in the closest collaboration with my own. together for f duri Dr. Collins'
on

senting the s of bot s, oocup f the area. He would be informed of r decision. Dr. Collins was not present at the talk but collaborated fully in all that followed.

We decided to lay the matter the next day before the lst Army G. 2 at Weimar and to ask for their approval to negotiate with the man for the unearthing of the films and their transfer with him to our HQ at

TOP SECRET

Molotov signs the secret agreement as Ribbentrop, standing behind him, and Stalin, in tunic, look on.

In 1943 German officials began scattering the foreign office's archival records. In 1945 they ordered all its documents to be destroyed.

That February Carl von Loesch, an interpreter for the foreign ministry, was sent to Thuringia to look after the most secret documents.

When the Allies suddenly advanced, he was ordered to destroy the archives. Defying the order, he saved 20 rolls of film with photographs of 9,725 pages of files, including this secret agreement, and buried the cache in Thuringia.

As luck would have it, I ran into our British chief, Col. R. C. Thomson of the Foreign Office, and we were approached by a German, Carl von Loesch, who claimed to be related to Churchill and who said he could take us to the place where microfilm of some of the most important documents of the German Government were buried. In return he wanted to be allowed to go with the film to London, saying he was the only one who could put the films together properly.

Col. Thomson did not want to make a decision without command approval, so he and I drove to Leipzig, the 7th Army Headquarters. There we got approval to deal with von Loesch, who then took us to a woods in Thüringen, north of Nordhausen, where we dug up a can of microfilm.

It contained the first copy that came into Allied possession of the secret protocol of the Molotov-Ribbentrop pact, signed August 23, 1939. This had to do with how the Germans and the Russians would divide Poland between them.

The pact led directly to the German attack on Poland. Stalin denied having made a pact with Germany, and von Loesch had been ordered to destroy this copy of the protocol. Instead he buried it along with other documents.

I took other trips on such matters, one of which took me to Munich and Rosenheim, where by chance I found the Kloeck family, with whom I had lived in Munich in 1932-33. Their place in Munich was bombed out. Their daughter "Motti" was married to Werner Hucke, who had become a German citizen.

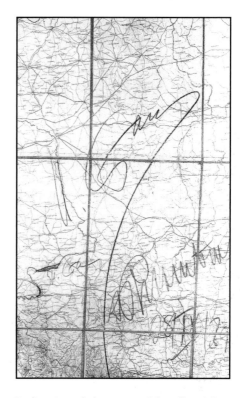

Stalin signed the map with a flourish and drew a line through Poland along the Narew, Vistula, and San Rivers. Russia was to get the land to the east, including Lithuania, Latvia, Estonia, and Finland. Ribbentrop's signature is at lower right.

The Molotov-Ribbentrop Pact

The Molotov-Ribbentrop pact was the single most important diplomatic event preparing the way for World War II. In August 1939, the Soviet Union and Nazi Germany negotiated a treaty in which they agreed not to attack each other; and furthermore to divide up eastern Europe into their respective spheres of influence.

In September 1939, Germany and the USSR attacked Poland, and World War II began. Stalin and Hitler decided the agreement but it was known by the names of the Soviet Foreign Minister, V.M. Molotov, and the German Foreign Minister, Joachim von Ribbentrop.

Why did they do this? After all, Communists and Nazis were sworn enemies. But diplomacy overrides ideology, and both Stalin and Hitler were skilled negotiators and practitioners of what is called realism in international relations (in German, *Realpolitik*).

Hitler realized that Germany lacked the economic and military resources to fight England, France, and Russia all at once. (He did not worry about the US because during the 1930s it was strongly neutralist and isolationist.)

Like every German state of the previous 100 years, Nazi Germany worried about an alliance between Russia and France that would threaten Germany with a two-front war; so Hitler hoped for an alliance with England (such as the Anglo-Prussian alliance which had defeated Napoleon). But in the late 1930s, as relationships with England turned increasingly hostile, Hitler began secret negotiations with Russia.

Why did Stalin respond?

Many in the capitalist democracies of the West regarded the Soviet Union as their greatest enemy, threatening to bring about Communist revolution everywhere. The USSR was trying to build itself from a backward agrarian society into an industrial economy, but it still needed a breathing space to catch up.

The USSR had no allies and had even been excluded from the Munich Conference in 1938, in which the Western powers agreed to allow Hitler to annex the German-speaking parts of Czechoslovakia in return for a promise to seek no further expansion.

When Hitler started sending feelers through diplomatic channels in Berlin and the German embassy in Moscow, Stalin saw an opportunity to make a deal with the devil. Fearing that Hitler would eventually attack Russia, Stalin would have liked an alliance with England and France, but that was not going to happen.

Hitler's offer gave Stalin a chance for the necessary breathing space to build up his military, while hoping that the Germans would fight the French and English, preferably in a long drawn-out war that would bleed both of them to death.

Stalin got his breathing space, but it wasn't as long as he had expected. In May 1940, Hitler attacked France; but instead of a long war, the Blitzkrieg (lightning war) of the German tank attack rapidly broke through the French lines and conquered the entire country within two months. Germany and England engaged in a year of aerial warfare (the Battle of Britain), which proved a stalemate; so Hitler finally turned back to attack Russia in June 1941.

At the end of the war, Ralph Collins participated in the discovery and acquisition of the microfilm which contained the actual text of the Molotov-Ribbentrop pact.

Why was this still important?

In May 1945, in the wake of Germany's collapse, Soviet forces were occupying eastern Europe, and a struggle was starting over which of these states would go to the Communist bloc, which would go to the Western anti-Communist bloc, and which would remain neutral (as Austria eventually did). The Americans, British, and Russians were engaged in redrawing the map of Europe.

The Western powers of course knew about the Molotov-Ribbentrop pact, but not its secret protocol specifying how Russia and Germany planned to parcel out these territories. Thus the agreement that Stalin had made with the Nazis was crucial evidence that could be used against him. Digging up the microfilm was a piece of the Cold War that was now beginning.

Randall Collins

Above: Marburg Castle.

Below: Great Knight's Hall in 2005. Ralph's group worked here in warm weather.

After about a month of running around, my group settled down in Marburg on the Lahn. The American forces had captured the Archives of the German Foreign Office in Thüringen, an area that was to become part of the Soviet Zone, and so the Americans moved the Archives to the Castle in Marburg.

Our group lived in a German Student Fraternity, just below the Castle. We set up our desks and the British Air Force microfilm unit and its equipment in the Great Knight's Hall, der Grosser Rittersaal.

We had German assistants who were familiar with the files bring us the material we wanted to look at. We chose the pages we wanted microfilmed.

I was the one who insisted that we needed a system of identification for our material. This consisted of each researcher listing the important documents on an accompanying typed sheet, on which the microfilmers would enter the microfilm serial numbers.

So, if you examine a copy of *Nazi-Soviet Relations 1939-1941*, you will see at the beginning of each item something like "Frames 210475-210476, serial 380." Of course the index sheets sent to Washington and London would also show that this was a Very Urgent telegram from Ribbentrop to Schulenberg, the German Ambassador in Moscow.

It would also indicate briefly the matter discussed. I am sure that I made the job for researchers much easier by insisting that we adopt some such method of identification.

Painting of Marburg Castle.

Pre-war map of Germany. Dörnbach is in the southwest corner (arrow).

When cool weather came, the Marburg group moved into the Martin Luther Room at the Castle. It had heat, whereas der Grosser Rittersaal had none.

Several weeks after my arrival in Germany and while I was visiting our main office in Hoechst, I asked whether I could have a car and chauffeur to take me down into the Rheinpfalz, in the French Occupied Zone. One of the secretaries said she would like to go along. We drove through Mainz and Bad Kreuznach down to Rockenhausen.

My wife's uncle, Richard Zubiller, and his family lived in the small town of Dörnbach, just a mile or so from Rockenhausen. We found Onkel Richard's place – he ran a Wirtschaft – an inn with a bar – on the main street through town. They were overjoyed to meet me and we had a good visit.

Then Onkel Richard suggested we go over to Alzey to visit an aunt. I had to walk down the street to the French commandant of the town and get permission for Maria's uncle to go with us to Alzey. Anyhow, it was a great pleasure for us both to go to Alzey and meet the aunt. This was the beginning of my acquaintance with Maria's relatives.

Tante Auguste Zubiller welcomes Ralph to Dörnbach in Sept. 1945 and gives him a photo of Karoline Zubiller, Maria's grandmother. Richard's daughter Renate is on the far left.

Dearest Maria,

Germany
May 11, 1945

I was in Wiesbaden only one night. We were in a very nice hotel there, but the upper stories were damaged from bombing. We had a very nice trip from there to where we are now. . . .Except for a few tanks and trucks destroyed here and there along the road, you wouldn't have known that there had been any war.

It's quite a different matter in the cities. Kassel, for instance, is an awful mess from the air bombing. The main part of the city is almost rubble. . . .

Germany
May 13, 1945

I have been traveling pretty steadily the last few days. . . .I have seen more of Thüringen. I met, quite by accident, the British team leader, Dr. Thomson, and I have been with him two days now. We were in the Eastern Harz Mts. Since then we have been in Weimar, which is pretty well torn up.

I hope before long to go to Marburg, where we shall pretty soon be well established. It wouldn't be such a bad place to live, don't you think so? There was only a little bombing there, around the railroad, and the rest is intact. I'll write you more when I know more, and when I feel I can tell more.

May 16, 1945

I am sorry I didn't get the above mailed, but I have been in the midst of a most unusual adventure, of story-book kind, and I have not been able to mail it. The adventure will have to wait for telling because it involves matters of utmost secrecy.

In the meantime I have seen Marburg and the set-up will be very nice, except that at present it is a little crowded. Kassel must be about the sorriest sight in Germany. In the center of the city there is utter destruction. I am never two days in the same place, but I hope some day to get a letter from you.

Germany
May 30, 1945

I have been investigating potash mines, but I haven't had to go down into any yet. That may be necessary at some places. I was in an underground factory a few days ago. Nearby was a concentration camp. There was enough evidence of mistreatment to make us wait until we were well away before eating our lunch.

I have listened to some very interesting stories by Germans recently. It is especially interesting to see what future they think Germany has. Among other interesting things at the present time is the reaction of Germans to Berlin broadcasts. They hear the Philharmonic and other things which make them wonder whether they should have feared the Russians so much. A few days ago I saw a trainload of Russian civilian workers leaving for Russian territory.

I just left base yesterday morning to travel in a slightly different region. I'll be able to mention some of the places soon in my letters. One thing that seems to be different is the military government set-up. Also, we had difficulties getting a billet last night, that is, my negro driver and I. . . . I have been called to breakfast. . . .

I certainly hope you have been getting my mail. So far, I have not had any of your letters at all. . . .By the way, I am near Kassel, a little to the East. You may have guessed it. I think we are now free to say where we are.

Germany
June 2, 1945

I recently saw Hildesheim. It had been one of my favorite cities. It is now practically a pile of rubble. They were still pulling down walls and clearing the streets. Later, I was in a potash mine where the art treasures from the museum and cathedral in Hildesheim were stored. Yesterday I was in another potash, or salt, mine. We had to climb up ladders for 115 meters, so it was rather strenuous. The finds were not worth the trouble. They included the Góttingen library stored in a mine gallery.

There has been a terrible lack of coordination in the job to which I am assigned. I am doing my best. I have the wonderful satisfaction of having had a part in one of the most important finds to be made in our field. I don't know whether the straight story will ever get into the newspapers, but the matter is now already in the hands of the very top men in the U.S. & British gov'ts. There was some account in *Stars & Stripes* of a find, which sounds like a garbled account of the real story. I have already mentioned it to you before, and some day I shall tell you all the details.

Love, Ralph

Ambassador Robert Murphy, Ralph's boss during this European tour of duty. Murphy's title at this time was US Political Adviser for Germany, SHAEF. The title belied the actual scope of his work and his influence on international affairs.

Left to right: General Sir Brian Robertson, British Military Governor, Germany; Charles E. Bohlen, later the US ambassador to the Soviet Union; General Vasily Chuikov, Russian Military Governor, Germany; and Robert Murphy.

Robert Murphy entered the State Department in 1917 and pursued a diplomatic career in Europe. After France fell in 1940, President Roosevelt turned Murphy from a conventional diplomat into a secret agent, to report directly to Roosevelt on the conflicts among the factions – Vichy, neutral, and free French – in French North Africa, and to line up support for the Allied invasion of Africa.

Murphy reported directly to Roosevelt and carried out his orders outside the chain of command, sometimes bypassing his superiors in the State Department. Murphy coordinated US diplomacy with Allied military operations during the invasion of Italy and the conquest of Germany. He won a reputation for getting things done in adverse and murky situations.

The cooperation Murphy improvised between diplomats and the military was to become a basic policy of the State Department. Eventually Murphy carried out special and undocumented missions not only for Roosevelt but also for Presidents Truman and Eisenhower. Much of his work was undocumented until he wrote *Diplomat among Warriors*, published in 1964.

Dearest Maria,

Our last trip was completed with beautiful weather to the end. We had lots of wonderful scenery, and we were also able to get something done.

Hitler's place above Berchtesgaden is quite a scene of destruction, and is swarming with Americans to see the sights. I was amazed at the size of the whole establishment. Besides Hitler's, Bormann's and Goering's houses, there were police barracks, SS barracks and enough other large buildings to make it a very large place.

We spent a very interesting evening on the hill and in the castle in the center of Kufstein. The Austrians hope to profit by a separation evidently, but are afraid of the Russians, like all other Germans. They have had so much propaganda against the Russians that it is small wonder that they believe the worst.

For the second time, I saw some Germans I had known in 32-33. They were the Klőcks with whom I had lived in Munich. The father had a very good business as Apotheker in the town. The mother was in Munich so I didn't get to see her. The daughter was there. Their home was in the outskirts of Berlin and she had left there the middle of Feb. with her two children to come south. The younger couple were of course very much upset because of losing everything, but he hoped for a job.

In a few days I expect to be back at headquarters. Certainly by then there should be some mail waiting for me. It seems an awfully long time, and I just hope there has been no delay with my letters to you.

I feel awfully sorry that you have had no answers from me to all your letters, but not until two days ago did I get any of your mail, and then only the one of June 11. In it you spoke of your sailing plans. Assuming that possibly you had not gotten my letters on the advisability of waiting, I sent the cable off yesterday. Today I got 13 letters from you: Mar. 28, 30, Apr. 3, 4, 7, 9, 12-16, 26, 30, May 1, 4, 7, June 5. Since there are some missing toward the end, I don't know what your decisions have been. From your last [June 11] letter, I presume you are coming on to London, and from the June 5 letter I assume you may be waiting in Cornwall to hear from me.

If the cable reaches you before too late, then you may decide, from this letter and what I can find out right away, what you want to do. From your reaction to my end of April and early May letters, I see that you would be awfully disappointed not to make the trip this summer. The only bad thing is that I have done nothing to make it simpler for you in London – house, etc. France is unadvisable, because of the food situation. Germany is out of the question until it has been officially ruled by military authorities that families may enter. When that happens, I shall want you to come directly to me. The only other possibility is London or suburbs.

If you decide to come to London, you might plan on staying at a family hotel in S. Kensington or thereabouts, where there are small parks for the children, etc. Accommodations on arrival are taken care of by the Embassy. If they prove too expensive, you can look around as I suggest. The furniture you could leave stored in N.Y. or send it to London for storage. That can be taken care of thru the embassy. Mr. Rice in the finance office is most helpful and efficient. Also thru the embassy you can get help in locating a house or flat. Mrs. Wiesner will be most helpful.

If it is at all possible, I should come to London as soon as possible, and help out as much as I can. If only we could have exchanged ideas a little more easily, it would not now be such an uncertainty.

As for money, if you leave, be sure to notify the State Dept. that your allowance should be paid thru the London Embassy. Also, bring your bills to Mr. Rice. If they have to be sent to me, he will tell you. I now have a $200 check which I shall hold until I know where you will be. It will help you out. Also, another check should be ready for me now. I will save them both.

It was wonderful to read all your letters. I did it very hurriedly, just before lunch today. I shall reread them more leisurely later. It made me feel so good to read of all the doings of the children. I should so much love to see them. The pictures are wonderful to have.

You seem to have managed wonderfully. You are a most wonderful wife, and I am proud of you. It will not be long before we shall see each other.

Love, Ralph

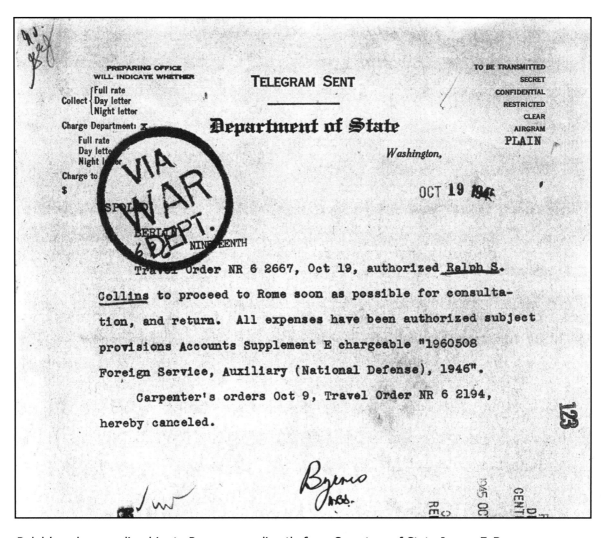

TELEGRAM SENT

Department of State

Washington,

OCT 19 1946

NINETEENTH

Travel Order NR 6 2667, Oct 19, authorized Ralph S.

Collins to proceed to Rome soon as possible for consulta-

tion, and return. All expenses have been authorized subject

provisions Accounts Supplement E chargeable "1960508

Foreign Service, Auxiliary (National Defense), 1946".

Carpenter's orders Oct 9, Travel Order NR 6 2194,

hereby canceled.

Byrnes

123

Ralph's orders sending him to Rome came directly from Secretary of State James F. Byrnes.

Assignment: Rome

In October I received orders for temporary duty in Rome, to replace a US officer at the Embassy who had to return to the States for family matters. The job was similar to the one I was doing in Marburg, except that the documents were those of Mussolini and the Fascist Party.

Because I had expected to be in Rome only a month to six weeks, I did not undertake any special investigation of my own, but cooperated very closely with our British counterparts at the document center. There, as in Marburg, I got accustomed to the English custom of mid-morning and -afternoon tea.

Being in Rome again reminded me of my student days, when I had fallen in love with Italy, except that this time I lived first at the new hotel Mediterraneo, and then for a while at the old Savoia.

I had a fine opportunity to get acquainted with Italian opera. I attended many great performances, highlighted by a *Norma* with Maria Caniglia, soprano, and Ebe Stignani, contralto. Both were superb singers; I have never heard a better contralto than Stignani. I also had the opportunity of visiting all the wonderful sights of Rome and its surroundings.

On one occasion (February 18-28, 1946) I even had a trip to Bolzano and Ortisei in the Italian Alps. My love for Italy was greatly enhanced. In March I traveled to Siena, Florence, Livorno – all in just three days.

At the time I went into the Foreign Service, I said that I wanted to take the examinations for career service. Examinations were announced for November 1945. When I was sent to Italy, it was arranged that I would take the Foreign Service examination in Naples. Most of the people taking the examination were in the military service.

The examination covered three days. Although it was quite an ordeal, I felt that I had done very well. As a matter of fact, in the mathematical part I had time to check carefully, and I knew that I had made no mistakes.

I was therefore horrified to learn in March 1946, that the Department had not looked at my examination – they had given me the wrong test, the one designed for the military alone. The Ambassador said I should draft a telegram of protest to the Department and that he would sign it.

That didn't change anything, but they did give me a special examination in June 1946, designed for all those who were in the same situation as I.

Entrance to Ralph's office in Berlin.
The sign reads:
7771 Document Center
Ministerial Documents Branch
Machine Tabulations Branch
Central Registry of War Criminals
and Security Suspects Branch

Managing and moving 500 tons of documents

After his initial assignment in 1945, securing Nazi documents as the Allies secured towns in Germany, Ralph was put in charge of documents collected at Marburg Castle. This work was part of a close collaboration between the British Foreign Office and US State Department (FO/SD) Documents Unit. Col.Thomson headed the British side of the FO/SD.

In October 1947, Ralph became a Foreign Service Officer and was promoted to head the US side of the FO/SD. To summarize his work up to the time of his promotion, Ralph wrote a ten-page memorandum to his boss, Robert Murphy, on January 29, 1948.

In the memorandum Ralph stated that every year his Unit had moved 500 tons of documents to a new location. In May 1945, many of the documents had been accumulated by the Allies at various castles -- Meisdorf, Degenershausen, Falkenstein, Marburg.

In February 1946, all the documents had to be moved again and were consolidated in an old building at Berlin's Tempelhof Airport. This building proved as impossible to heat as Marburg Castle had been, as the plumbing pipes were completely frozen in the airport building and in the underground passages at the airport.

The documents were finally moved to a modern and attractive building at the Documents Center at Krumme Lanke, in southwest Berlin. These moves entailed "52 ten-ton trailer loads of documents, 25 loads of shelves, 8 loads of furniture, and 9 loads of library books."

The Archives consisted of many collections: political files dating back to 1936; files of the Office of the Reichsminister [Ribbentrop] and Staatssekretär [Secretary of State], from 1920 to 1936; files from the Weimar Republic, 1919-1933, which had been badly damaged when the truck trying to transport them from Berlin in 1944 was burned; files of the Schuldereferat and Parliamentary Investigation Committee; diplomatic files from various German embassies, legations, and consulates; files of Reichsminister Albert Speer; and many more.

Ralph was responsible for organizing and storing the archives in proper conditions. He had a staff of 2 American assistants and 36 German archivists.

Beginning in 1945, while the files were still at Marburg Castle, many nations sent missions to work with the documents, including France, Belgium, The Netherlands, Czechoslovakia, Denmark, Luxembourg, and Norway.

One of these missions was the German War Documents Project, a historian-led project begun in November 1946 as a joint effort of the US State Department and the British Foreign Office. The most prominent of the visiting missions was the Office of the Chief of Council, War Crimes, which was assembling evidence to be used in the Nuremberg trials.

Assignment: Berlin

The six weeks I had expected to stay in Rome became six months. In mid-April I flew to Frankfurt and then to Berlin. The Marburg outfit – personnel and archives – had been moved to Berlin, and I went back to my previous assignment.

My main concern back in Berlin was to get my family to join me. I started looking for a house and was offered one. But I still didn't have permission for my family to travel to Berlin.

I finally talked to Mr. Heath, the Deputy Chief of Mission under Ambassador Robert Murphy, and he interceded in the matter – with success! And I got a better house, in the Dahlem section of Berlin. That was May 24, 1946. On the 27th and 28th I took the Foreign Service Exams.

I left immediately for Frankfurt and Paris to meet my family. They had arrived a day or two before me and were comfortably installed at the Hotel Crillon, which had been assigned to the Americans at that time.

For me, it was a joyous occasion. I had not seen them in 14 months. We relaxed for a few days in Paris. The children played in the Tuileries and Luxembourg gardens. We took the train to Frankfurt, where we spent a couple of days, and then to Berlin, to the house I had rented at Am Erlenbusch No. 4. It was partly furnished, and our own furniture arrived quite promptly.

TELEGRAM SENT

4587

To: SECSTATE

Date: 24 April 1946

No.: 1098

Code: UNRESTRICTED

Charged to:
GPO 1-1142

Info:

FOR SHIPLEY FROM COLLINS

Mrs. Ralph Collins and children may obtain military permit to enter Germany at Paris. Please issue passports and visas carrying them to Paris so that they can make May first shipping date of S. S. Brazil as planned.

MURPHY

RLCollins/srd

OMGUS AG Pubs 747/25M/12/13/45

In Cornwall-on-Hudson, waiting to join Ralph in Europe.

The family actually sailed on the *S.S. Uruguay* on May 15.

The family reunited in Paris.

Berlin lay in ruins, with many streets impassable. Three-fourths of its housing was destroyed, and its people lived crowded into half-ruined rooms. Workers, mostly women, formed lines clearing rubble stone by stone, brick by brick, but barely making a dent in the mountains of rubble.

Buried deep within the East German sector under Soviet control, the people of West Berlin relied on the Western Allies to bring in all the food and supplies needed for mere survival. To live on the thin edge of survival was an exhausting feat. In winter, with almost no coal, people froze – 12,000 Berliners froze to death in the winter of 1947, the coldest winter in a century.

And all year they starved. Ration cards gave workers food but not enough to keep up their strength; the housewives' ration was so low it was called a death card. Crops failed. Packs of wolves roamed the streets at night along with women picking through garbage cans for food.

Berlin, once Europe's center of science and art, now was the crime capital, with a daily count of 240 robberies – most of which netted literally a few potatoes. Its citizens were described as "a ruined, poverty-stricken people, with little to eat, everything to fear, nothing to hope for."

We lived in the American Zone, in a three-story house with a nice backyard. The house had pockmarks on the front wall where exploding shells had hit it.

One afternoon Randy, then 5, was playing in the park across the street when he found a hand grenade. Delighted at his find, he came running into the house with it, yelling, "Mommy, Mommy, look what I found!" He was very upset when Mother took it away from him.

One day a Russian truck pulled up in front of the house next door. Randy, Mary, and I stood on the bottom rung of the fence between the two houses and watched as the Russian soldiers dug up a body from the garden. It was a Russian soldier, and this was a day when the Russians were allowed into the American Zone to reclaim their war dead.

When we went to the parks to play, Mother did not allow us to play on the grass. The Army had not yet cleared out the land mines, so Mother insisted that we play on the sidewalks. The widest sidewalks were around the equestrian statues, and that's where we were ordered to stay. Twenty years passed before I realized why my blood boiled whenever I passed an equestrian statue!

Erica

The Nuremberg Trials

After the end of World War II, war crimes trials were held for the most important captured leaders of Nazi Germany. An International Military Tribunal was presided over by four judges from Britain, the United States, France, and Russia, and with prosecutors from these four countries, the occupying forces in Germany. The city of Nuremberg was chosen because it was a favorite city for Nazi party rallies.

The main trial took place from November 20, 1945 to October 1, 1946, during which time 24 prominent Nazis were tried, including Martin Bormann, Herman Göring, Alfred Rosenberg, and Joachim von Ribbentrop, all of whom were found guilty and sentenced to death.

Ralph Collins' investigations of Foreign Ministry documents were instrumental in the case against von Ribbentrop, the former Foreign Minister. Ralph was invited to attend the trials, which was one of many major historical events he witnessed during his diplomatic career.

Randall Collins

Except for the fact that the weather in Berlin was much cooler than in the States, the children adapted well, and we were all happy. We had a housekeeper and a maid, and the children soon learned enough German to get whatever they needed.

A visitor from Czechoslovakia, Professor Svoboda, encouraged Maria and me to visit Prague, which we enjoyed. This was before Czechoslovakia became a Communist state.

At the German Foreign Office Archives, where I was to work for the next two years, I found my old German professor, John T. Krumpelmann, who had been my second teacher at the University of North Carolina in 1927. He and his British wife were a happy addition to our job associates. Ted Reynolds was still on the job. New to our outfit was William P. Cumming, Professor of English at Davidson College. Bill had volunteered for service in Japan, where he had lived as a boy. He was surprised to be sent to Germany instead, but he was a capable and worthy addition to our staff.

The Collins' house in Berlin.

The more unusual additions were two History professors, Dr. Fritz Epstein from Stanford and Dr. Raymond Sonntag from the University of California. They actually were not part of our team; that is, they did not work for the Department of State, but were invited in to write the history of German diplomatic relations in the pre-World War II period.

We also had French participants in our research in the German archives. Our research was very helpful to the prosecutors for the Nuremberg trials, and I was invited to visit the tribunal.

Ralph reviewing documents.

Ralph, left, and colleagues.

As a family we settled down to what could be called normalcy. Erica and Randall went to the new American school (second grade and kindergarten).

We had our own car to drive in town, and we were able to take a few trips, with car and chauffeur, down into the French Zone, where we visited with Maria's kin in the Rheinpfalz. Maria went a few times by train down to her relatives. The trains were very crowded and had not been fully repaired – windows were broken, etc.

Our housekeeper, Frau Thiermann, was a very fine woman and very capable. There was usually a maid to assist her. One was a Yugoslav who had been with the Partisan troops in Yugoslavia.

Our house was ample and comfortable. It had not been damaged by the bombing and street fighting, although in the early months of our occupancy a group of Russian soldiers appeared and dug up one of their dead buried in the garden next door from the days of street battle in the city. Also, one day while the children were playing in the adjacent park, they found an unexploded hand-grenade. A call to the American Military Police took care of the grenade.

There were, of course, mountains of rubble, especially in the center of the city. It was a common sight to see women working away on the piles of bricks and stones, chipping away the mortar so the bricks and stones could be used again.

Our social life in Berlin was quite active. We frequently attended performances at the City Opera, and we even got to know some of the theater people.

Ralph (right) skiing with friends.

Berlin's buildings, many in ruins, stood in a sea of rubble. Citizens, mostly women, ceaselessy worked to clear the rubble. It was carried away by hand by long chains of Berliners who cleaned the city brick by brick. In 1948 many streets still were not passable.

The mountains of rubble were estimated at almost 2 billion cubic feet, and in 1948, after three years of hard work, not even five percent of the rubble had been cleared away. It was 1988 before the last broken window was replaced.

Many parts of Germany, however, were spared, such as Dörnbach, where both of Maria's parents were born.

Dörnbach was a village surrounded by fields. Zubiller families worked in their fields but lived in town, in houses with adjoining stables for their farm animals.

The Gasthaus was owned by Richard Zubiller, seen above with his daughter, Renate, at the window at left; his wife, Lisa, is at the right window; and their son Erich stands next to the cow-drawn cart, at the entrance to the courtyard (at this time, in 1946, son Werner was still a Russian prisoner of war).

At right: Ralph's children in the courtyard in 1946.

One day our boxer Bonzo disappeared. Our house was opposite a park. A block away was Schorlemer Allee, a huge divided highway on which roamed huge double-decker buses, like those in London, only the German buses were painted khaki color.

Mary Johanna was quite young at that time, about 4. She liked to walk around the block. When she wanted to go for a walk, she wanted somebody to go with her.

If she couldn't find somebody, she would take off by herself which frightened me and our housekeeper Frau Thiermann, and whatever maid we had at the time. We'd scatter and start looking for Mary.

One day she came home and said, "Mommy, I heard Bonzo." Mary spoke German quite fluently and she told Frau Thiermann, who told our houseman, an elderly German man who took care of the coal furnace and the grounds, to go out with Mary and see if he could find out if it was our Bonzo.

So they went down the block and Mary pointed out the house across the street. Fortunately she had not tried to cross the street herself. But she had heard a dog barking in the basement of this house and thought she recognized Bonzo's voice.

Our houseman went over and knocked on the door and said, "I hear you have a dog in your basement. I want to see the dog."

Well, of course, the Germans protested and said that they had a dog, but that it was their dog. Our houseman threatened to call the military police if they didn't show him the dog. This was just enough to frighten these people into bringing up the dog.

And sure enough, it was Bonzo.

Maria Collins

Our dog Bonzo in Berlin looked like this.

The family with Struppi, whose name means Little Mess.

134

We knew some of the ballet dancers. One in particular was Maria Litto, with her Swiss husband, Elimar. We had good times together and met a lot of people in the musical world. One night when we had a party at our house, thieves sat in our basement until some guests left and others had retired for the night and then stole some of the coats and things.

We had very good relations with our English colleagues. They invited us to their Blau-Weiss Club, and we invited them to Harnack House. One weekend in winter I went with my English colleagues to their rest and recreation center in the Harz Mountains for a weekend of skiing and relaxation.

We also had some French friends, especially a Captain Bernard Bonnafous, whom we frequently visited in the French Sector. One summer we went to his home in the Province of Aveyron, and we had a very interesting time visiting with some of his macqui friends who had been in the Resistance during the German occupation. These friends included the manager of the Roquefort cheese caves and industry, who gave us a very fine banquet. Bernard's father had been in the French diplomatic service.

One feature of life in Germany right after the war was the prevalence of the black market, in which American cigarettes became the currency of exchange. It seems that no one was interested in real money, due perhaps on the German side to their memory of inflation in the mid-1920s, when the German mark became practically worthless.

Many Americans profiteered from this situation. We did not want to participate, but

A visit to Zubiller relatives in the town of Schweissweiler. Maria is at far right, holding Mary.

sometimes it happened anyhow. When I had a Berlin tailor make me a suit, he insisted that he be paid in cigarettes – so for a couple of cartons I had a finely tailored suit.

While in Berlin I continued to concentrate on the documents in the German archives that had to do with the relations between Berlin and Moscow. Before leaving, I wrote a despatch to the Department summing up what I had found.

Dr. Epstein was especially complimentary on my despatch, saying that it was an excellent summary of Berlin-Moscow relations before the war and up to the German attack on the Soviet Union. I assume that it was on the basis of my work in the Archives that I was selected for Russian Language and Area Training, to be followed by an assignment to our Embassy in Moscow.

I received my orders for Moscow in April 1948. We left Berlin just before the Berlin Blockade. Our household goods were packed for shipment, and because the trains could not run, our goods had to be unpacked and flown to Frankfurt, where they were repacked for shipment to the States. As a result of all the repacking, we lost some things – I remember specifically a picture of Goethe and a reproduction of a painting by Dufy. Also we had quite a bit of breakage of glassware and the like.

We left Berlin by car, crossing the English Channel from Calais to Dover. We spent one night in Canterbury and two nights in London before taking a ship from Southampton to New York.

The Berlin Blockade

When World War II ended, the victorious powers divided Germany into four zones: Russian, British, French, and American. Because the powers failed to reach an agreement on the status of Berlin, it was also divided into four zones. But Berlin was entirely surrounded by the Russian zone, which later became East Germany – the DDR, or Deutsche Demokratische Republik. The Western powers were guaranteed access through the Russian zone by several highways.

The Cold War began in 1947 with tensions between the Russians and the Western Powers, including disagreements about how post-war Germany was to be reconstructed. At the end of March 1948, the Russians increasingly restricted access to Berlin, and by June 1948, they had closed down all rail and highway access to Berlin.

Ralph and his family left Berlin as the Berlin Blockade began. President Truman declared his unwillingness to withdraw from Berlin. An airlift was begun, supplying the military and civilians in the western zones of Berlin. The airlift continued until May 1949, when the Soviets relented and reopened the ground corridors.

Randall Collins

We left Berlin in April 1948. I don't remember whether it was by train or car, but we had diplomatic passports and the papers we needed to cross the border and leave the Russian Zone.

At the border crossing, however, we were detained for several hours. Dad had to go into an office and present our passports and papers for approval by the Russian authorities.

Mother stayed with us three kids and for once she was very subdued. This change from her usual behavior was not lost upon us kids, and for once we too kept still.

Erica

By spring of 1948, relations between the West and Russia had reached the breaking point. On June 24 the Russians blockaded all ground transport to Berlin and surrounded the city with an army and with trainloads of supplies to be distributed only if Berliners would accept Communist rule. With an eye on controling all of Europe, Russia expected to starve and freeze West Berlin into submission.

President Truman and the State Department saw only two options: to send an armored column into West Berlin, most likely to result in another major war, or to abandon Berlin to the Russians, which would destroy America's reputation throughout Europe.

Armed with only a few small planes, Gen. Lucius Clay started to airlift food, fuel, medical supplies, and other essentials into Berlin. The pilots flew from US air bases in West Germany and over an East Germany corridor 20 miles wide, harassed by Russian fighter planes.

Nearly everyone believed it would be impossible to meet even the most minimal requirements for food and, particularly come winter, coal to a city of 2.5 million people who had been starving for three years.

President Truman supported the airlift, overruling his senior advisors. Gen. William Tunner, who had organized a similar feat from India to China in World War II, organized the flight plan so that 250 planes, nearly every available military transport, took off and landed every 3 minutes around the clock. Pilots from several nations flew at precise speeds and altitudes in order to make 480 flights daily. The airlift saved West Berlin and checked Soviet expansion into Western Europe, thus helping Truman win the 1948 election.

In 1948, in a bitterly harsh winter, 85% of West Berliners voted to reject Communism in favor of democracy and to turn for help to the Allies, who three years before had bombed Berlin into ruins. This courage and conviction is what led President Kennedy to say in 1963, "*Ich bin ein Berliner!*"

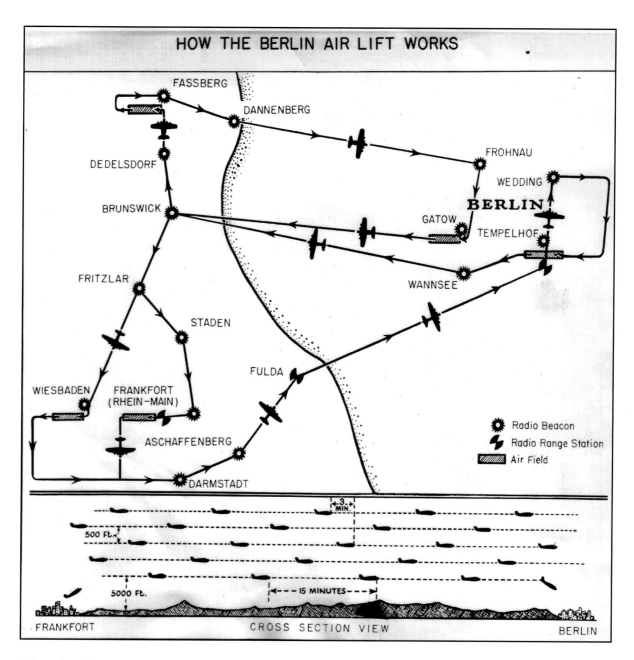

When this diagram was made, planes took off and landed at 15-minute intervals.

Year in the States

After a brief vacation, I was busy studying Russian at the Foreign Service Institute in Washington DC. Actually, I had begun teaching myself Russian while at Maryville College, in the early part of the war. I did not have a teacher, however, until I was in Berlin in 1946. For part of the summer of 1948 I was alone in Washington, but a professor at the Institute let me have his house during the month of August, so the whole family came down to Washington.

In September I went to the Russian Institute at Columbia University. Three of us who were destined for Moscow were there together. I lived in the Faculty house, Butler Hall, just off the Columbia campus. I had a bachelor apartment, but spent every weekend with my family in Cornwall-on-Hudson, where they were living with Maria's parents, Alfred and Maria Zubiller. The Westside railway made it easy to commute, but most frequently Maria drove me back to the City on Sunday afternoon.

Among my professors at the Russian Institute were Dr. Geroid Robinson, Russian History, later the Institute Director; Abram Bergson, Economics; Ernest J. Simmons, Russian Literature; and John N. Hazard, Russian Politics, who had started the Institute. At the end of the year, I wrote a paper, "Soviet View of the Colonial Problem since the Varga Controversy." It was published by the Department of State, Foreign Service Institute Monograph Series No. 2, June 1949.

Central Moscow, showing site of US Embassy and Ambassador's residence.

Москва. Улица Горького.

Gorky Street, with the Historical Museum ahead in the distance. The US embassy was beyond and to the right.

Assignment: Moscow

In April 1949 I received my orders to go to Moscow as Third Secretary, Vice-Consul, and FSO-6. After much consultation about what to take with us, especially canned goods, we left for Moscow in early July, on the *Gripsholm*.

Landing in Göteborg, we went by train to Stockholm, where we waited several days for a Russian ship, the *Byeli-Ostrov*, to take us to Leningrad by way of Helsinki.

We enjoyed our trip across the Atlantic, especially the day along the northern coast of Scotland, and our stay in Stockholm, where we visited the parks and other places of interest to us and to the children. We went ashore in Helsinki and then continued on the ship overnight to Leningrad. After a night and day in Leningrad, we took an overnight train to Moscow.

We were met at the Moscow train station by someone from the Embassy. We had lunch with the Ambassador, Admiral Alan G. Kirk, who had been in charge of the American landings on Omaha and Utah Beaches on D-Day.

After lunch we were taken to our house, 10 miles from the Embassy, because the apartments at the Embassy were not large enough for our family. Our house was an old dacha, or summer cottage, in what had once been the countryside but now was within the city limits.

When we arrived at the dacha, we kids took a quick look around the house. Then we went outside to explore. Our cook and housekeeper, Hilda, lived behind the garage with her three children: a boy 11, a girl 9, and a boy 4.

While we were exploring the yard, the girl came up to me with a ball in her hand and said, *"Hochesh eegrat v myach?"*

She repeated this over and over until I realized that she was saying, "Do you want to play ball?" And that's how I learned a lot of Russian.

Erica

The dacha was on Pervaya Ostankinskaya Street, near Ostankino Palace and a Park of Culture and Rest. Also near the dacha was a permanent Agriculture Exhibit, a large area to show off Soviet achievements in farming.

The house was not overlarge: a living room with a piano, a kitchen, a small dining room large enough only for the dining table and chairs, a fairly large bedroom, and a smaller bedroom. There was an enclosed porch off the smaller bedroom, but it was unheated and we could not use it. So the three children were a little crowded in one small bedroom with bunk beds.

The heating system was by hot-water radiators, with a furnace under the house. There was also a fairly large attic area, where we stored our canned goods and where the children played in bad weather. There was an electric hot-water heater for the bath.

We had a fairly large garden, with a strawberry patch, raspberry bushes, three kinds of currants – red, yellow and white – and an outdoor root cellar, which we didn't use. In the back was a garage with a room. Our housekeeper, Hilda, lived in that one room with her three children. They regarded it a great privilege because they had the room all to themselves. We also had a maid, Galya, and a *dvornik*, a yard man, who also chopped wood and loaded coal in the furnace.

Luckily for Maria, Hilda was a Volga German, so they understood each other right away. Later Maria learned Russian and could do a lot of her own shopping.

Passport photo taken in spring 1949: Erica is 9, Randall is 7½, and Mary Johanna is 5½.

Dear Flo and Andy,

Hotel Regina, Stockholm, Sweden

July 21, 1949

I've sent cards but want to get this note off before we sail tomorrow on the Russian ship. There will be another couple and 2-year-old son and a single man going with us. I've been assured the ship is clean, the food good. Just in case – I've got a few extra groceries I can get at easily.

By good luck, met the couple en route to Washington whose house we'll have in Moscow. Have been assured the house is O.K. – but will be redecorated and repaired before winter. Garden large and well planted so should have plenty of fresh veg. & fruits until fall.

Have enjoyed our stay here but everything is expensive. Local foods are reasonable altho 1 orange or 1 peach costs about 30 cents. Will write in detail later.

Children enjoying the sights but still as blasé as ever about their surroundings. As long as they can buy comic books and ice cream cones or Good Humors on a stick they're happy. And there are plenty of both here. Randall supplied the Swedish elevator boy on the Gripsholm with Roy Rogers comics – it's not just National, it's an International craze.

Before I forget – took the children to see some American cartoons and comedies, including Laurel & Hardy, Charlie Chaplin, Leon Errol, Ben Turpin, Ed Kennedy – real oldies but just as funny as ever. They loved them.

When we get to Moscow, I'll send you our street address so you can write directly using 5 cents postage or 15 cents airmail. This is for letters only and with only non-political topics. It's quicker than by pouch through Washington. Our Washington address is: R.S. Collins, Foreign Service Mail Room, Dept. of State, Washington 25, D.C. (Moscow Pouch)

Hope you all are well. . . .Love from us all

P.S. Believe it or not, Randall has been the least trouble so far. Erica & Mary into mischief most of time. Keep busy washing & ironing for them.

We arrived here as expected 3 weeks to the day after we left New York. And within a day after our arrival we received your note and Lamar's card forwarded from Cornwall. . . .

We were fortunate to have beautiful weather all the way and during our week in Stockholm. We left Sweden on a Soviet ship which was immaculately clean and the food excellent. Of course I'd stocked up in Sweden and then didn't need it.

There was no difficulty going through Customs in Leningrad. An "Intourist" girl took us to their hotel (Intourist – Russian travel agency) where we had a comfortable room for the evening until train time.

Welcomed here by big delegation from Embassy. Our house is of logs but so are most of others in the neighborhood. Live on outskirts north of the city near the beautifully preserved Ostankino palace. Have a large garden well planted but ill-kept – Gardener too lazy. We always seem to inherit wilderness gardens. Ralph & Misha (gardener) cutting hedge & transplanting berry bushes.

Children are delightfully happy. We (I) bought a German police dog from Ed Stevens, correspondent for Christian Science Monitor. Dog born in Berlin from dog whose owner was Randall's kindergarten teacher!!

About to acquire Eddy Gilmore's cook. He's with New York Herald Tribune. Have a maid Hilda who speaks German. She has 3 children – boy 4, girl 9, boy 11, and live over the garage. Husband?

All our things came right with us so have been able to get settled. There's a Baby Grand piano in the house so we feel lucky. House needs lots of repairs....

Have started our Sunday School using what materials I have. Very few other children here – all small but may ask them to join us.

Moscow is a big disappointment as a city. Streets are wide on the main avenues but houses all dilapidated. Workers' paradise with women doing the manual labor. Kremlin from a distance looks beautiful with its golden cupolas (domes). Understand we shall be able to take Kremlin tour in about a year. . . .

Love, Maria

Military adventurism portends nothing but catastrophe for the imperialists!

About to walk off a cliff, US General Douglas MacArthur carries an atom bomb in one hand and a sign in the other, "American world order." Note the destroyed symbols of the Nazi "new order" on the cliff face.

It is hard now to visualize the hostility, contempt, and dread with which Americans looked at Russia in the late 1940s. Americans quailed at the very thought of traveling to, much less living in, Moscow. The Soviet Union was considered the mortal enemy of the United States, a powerful and hostile state led by a half-mad dictator out to destroy us and conquer the world.

The cold war was not just a slogan. It was real. To win it, both the United States and Russia were using all the tools they had, except military force, against each other. The American public thought the Russians would attack the US whenever they thought they could get away with it. . . .

The only Westerners allowed to live in Russia were diplomats, a half-dozen newspaper correspondents, and unmasked Russian spies who had fled their own countries. Once in Russia, Westerners were watched closely, their living and business quarters bugged, their local servants all informers, and their movements tracked. We could not go more than 25 miles from Moscow without special permission from the Foreign Ministry. Even our private cars always had to have Russian chauffeurs who reported on our itinerary and conversation. The only Russians allowed to talk to us were selected Foreign Ministry officials, servants, shopkeepers, and the like, and those conversations had to be strictly business. No social contact was allowed. Violations could mean a one-way trip to Siberia for the Russian.

Lydia (Mrs. Alan) Kirk

Randall and Duce in the garden. Behind them are neighborhood houses.

We children spent most of our time – when we weren't at school – at the dacha. Fortunately we had a big yard to play in and children to play with. When it got dark, which happened quite early in the winter, we played inside.

We liked to hang out in the kitchen and watch Hilda cook over the coal- and wood-fired stove. We played board games like Monopoly and records on a Victrola.

I remember browsing for hours in the Compton Encyclopedia and in the Sears catalog – sort of like surfing the Net!

Erica

I remember walking from the dacha to the villages where Misha and Galya lived in rustic log houses without running water. Villagers drew water from a communal pump and used outhouses.

I, at age 10, thought we must be very rich because we had much better living conditions than they did.

Erica

Dvor, or yard.

Randall, Mary Johanna, and three kittens born March 17.

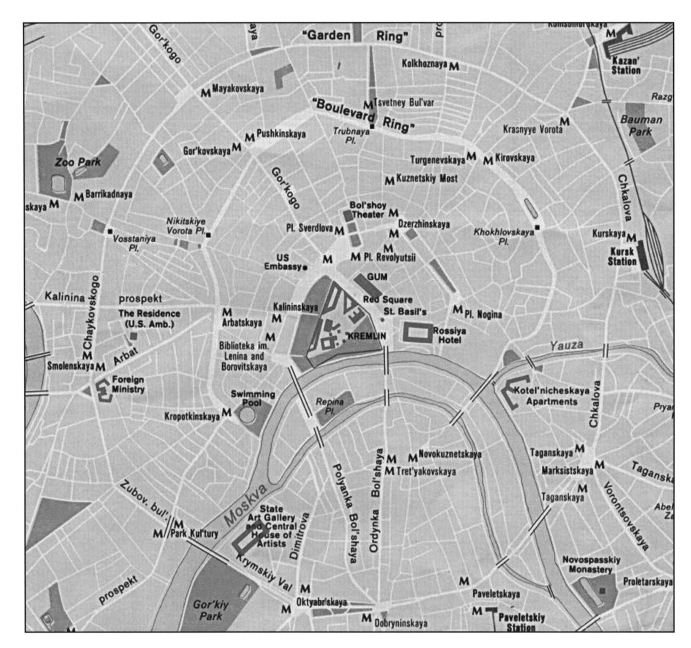

Moscow is laid out in concentric rings around the Kremlin. The US Embassy was near the northern tip of the Kremlin. On Kalinina prospekt, running west, was the Anglo-American School.

Maria had to work at the Embassy. There was not enough housing for Embassy secretaries, so wives had to work as secretaries or otherwise. Maria was first put in charge of the Embassy Commissary.

Then there arose the problem of school for the Embassy children, who previously had been allowed to attend Russian schools. We had taken along Calvert School materials for our three children. There were three other school-age children at the Embassy, and the decision was made to establish our own school.

The Military Attaché, Gen. "Mike" O'Daniel, had school equipment brought in by plane from Berlin. There were several British children of school age, so the British Embassy offered space in one of their buildings on Arbat Square.

Maria was put in charge of what became the Anglo-American School of Moscow. She taught first, third, and fifth grades – those which corresponded to all the children concerned. At the same time a kindergarten was established, which all the Western children in Moscow could attend, plus any non-Western Embassy children who could speak English. The school was a great success and is still operating in Moscow, with expanded faculty and facilities.

Our children soon learned Russian. They played hop-scotch and other games with Hilda's children and some of their neighborhood friends. The Embassy assigned a chauffeur and a car to take us to and from the Embassy every weekday and on other occasions. None of our Embassy people had private cars in Moscow.

In Red Square today, with the Kremlin on left and Historical Museum on right; the white building in the distance is the former US embassy.

For the school, Maria used materials from the Calvert School which she had brought to use with her children. Calvert is a private school in Baltimore that has served foreign diplomats and missionaries for decades.

At our little school, many late afternoons it became so cold that we had to bundle up in coats, scarves, and mittens. Our physical activities were necessarily inhibited by all this extra clothing, and we spent our time in endless spelling bees, which did not require writing or turning pages – hard to do wearing gloves or mittens.

The Calvert home schooling program included small books with spelling lists. The English kids were expected to provide the English spelling; we American kids were expected to spell it our usual way. But your mother often challenged us to provide the variant spelling for extra credit (spelling "labor" first l-a-b-o-r and then l-a-b-o-u-r).

The spelling bees occurred several times a week, always late in the afternoon – the final activity of the day. I suspect we were waiting for our parents to finish work at the embassies so we would return home together.

George Service, third-grade classmate

To help us kids build our Russian vocabulary, Dad bought two volumes of *Picture Dictionary of the Russian Language, a Study Aid for Pupils of Non-Russian Primary Schools,* published in 1949 for school children in Soviet republics where Russian was not the native language.

The illustrations in these books give the best idea of what Moscow looked like when we were there, including the sketch of the yard on page 153, as it was forbidden to take photographs anywhere but at the dacha and on embassy property.

Photographs taken in Moscow even a decade later do not show the city as we knew it.

Erica

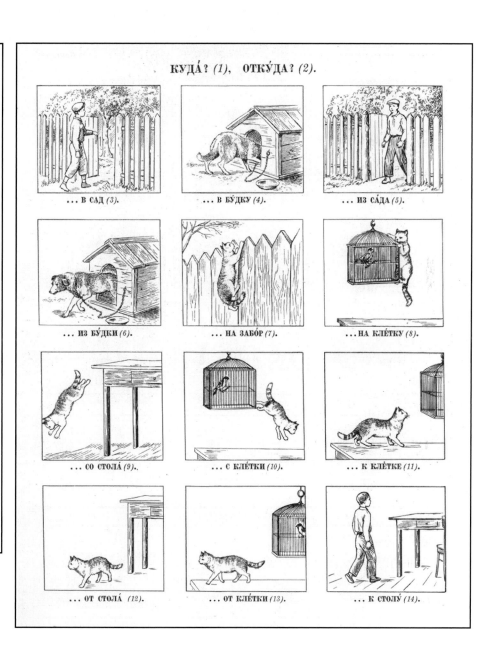

КУДА́? *(1)*, ОТКУ́ДА? *(2)*.

... В САД *(3)*.

... В БУ́ДКУ *(4)*.

... ИЗ СА́ДА *(5)*.

... ИЗ БУ́ДКИ *(6)*.

... НА ЗАБО́Р *(7)*.

... НА КЛЕ́ТКУ *(8)*.

... СО СТОЛА́ *(9)*.

... С КЛЕ́ТКИ *(10)*.

... К КЛЕ́ТКЕ *(11)*.

... ОТ СТОЛА́ *(12)*.

... ОТ КЛЕ́ТКИ *(13)*.

... К СТОЛУ́ *(14)*.

Anglo-American School of Moscow

When these pictures were taken in 2007, the School had grown to 1,400 students from 65 nations, pre-school to grade 12, with a waiting list of 250. The facility shown here opened in 2000.

Priority goes to children from British, US, and Canadian Embassies; next, to corporations from those nations; next, to other nations; and finally to Russian citizens. Annual tuition of $25,000 is paid by embassies and corporations; Russian citizens pay full tuition to attend this, Moscow's most prestigious school.

The School welcomed a visit by the first student of its first director. Left: Zhenya Ivanova, Assistant to the Director, greets Erica. Above: a pre-school class.

Above: Olympic-size pool. Below: cafeteria and an art class.

Above left: interior courtyard, with a wing for each school. Above right: the administrative wing.

Right: the playground is modeled after the Kremlin.

At the time it wasn't clear at all to me what my dad was doing. Sometimes late at night he got up and turned on the radio to listen to what the Soviet announcers were saying. It seemed to be his job to check up on the Russians.

Our parents never talked about politics. I had to figure things out for myself. I remember reading in *Stars and Stripes*, the newspaper published for the US military in Europe, that the Russians had shot down an American plane over the Baltic; war seemed imminent, but that crisis passed.

It must have been around the time the Korean War broke out that I noticed propaganda posters on walls. A poster image that sticks in my mind is the Statue of Liberty with chains around her neck and an American policeman hitting her over the head with his nightstick.

Randall

Each embassy in Moscow had to keep one or more foreigners to ride herd on the plumbers, electricians, painters, and carpenters that it employed. These workers were not typical, to be sure, as they probably had orders to work as little as possible in order to force us to employ more men and eventually cut the number of foreign personnel in order to save on costs.

Rev. Georges Bissonnette, US Chaplain

Spaso House, the US Ambassador's residence, 2007.

Former US Embassy; the 13 apartments on the lower floors were used for embassy offices, the commissary, and the doctor's and dentist's offices. The 17 apartments on the upper floors housed 47 embassy personnel. The apartment at top right corner has the balcony with the only view into Red Square.

My first assignment in Moscow was as Third Secretary and Vice-Consul. For the first few months I was in the Consular Section, under Charles Stefan, the Consul. I followed up on Embassy requests to the Soviet Foreign Office for permission for Russian wives of US citizens to go to America to join their husbands.

We were not very successful in this endeavor, and this problem of exit-visas for Russian wives of American citizens held several husbands in Moscow for quite a few years, in particular some Embassy employees and news correspondents.

It was only after Stalin died that the harsh Soviet attitude relaxed. Among the Russian wives were those of news correspondents Tom Whitney, Eddy Gilmore, and Ed Stephens, and also the wife of George Atkins, who was in charge of Embassy buildings and repairs.

In October 1949 I was assigned to the Public Affairs Office of the Embassy as Assistant PAO, and in April 1950 I became the Public Affairs Officer. In May of 1950 I was promoted to FSO-5 and Second Secretary of Embassy.

The Public Affairs job involved two special duties: monitoring Voice of America broadcasts to the Soviet Union and the publication and distribution of the Russian language magazine *Amerika*.

The former job involved having Embassy personnel on trips to other parts of the Soviet Union carry along radios and report on any reception of VOA broadcasts they were able to pick up.

Left: Embassy staff watch the parade on the Day of the Great October Socialist Revolution.
Right: The building is the Manège, which had been the horse barn of the Tsars.
Below: Tanks entering Red Square. The smoke is exhaust, not cannon fire!

Soviet law forbade the photographing of "military objectives," an undefined term. Therefore, the Embassy in Moscow prohibited the carrying of cameras. As a result, Dad rarely used his camera, and the only pictures we took were taken either at the dacha or from the one Embassy balcony with a view into Red Square.

Erica

The Soviet attempts to block reception were generally successful, but now and then we could report good reception outside Moscow.

The *Amerika* magazine took up the major part of my time. The articles for the magazine were written in Washington or New York and were sent to Moscow for translation into Russian. I had two Russian translators in my office plus typists and a messenger.

The translators brought me their translations, and I checked them for faithfulness to the English originals. The translators were excellent – they were professionals who not only translated from English but also produced Russian of good literary quality.

We sent the translations to New York, and the finished magazine was shipped to us in Moscow. We delivered it to Soyuzpechat, the Soviet agency for the distribution of magazines and other publications to newsstands throughout the Soviet Union.

When our Embassy people went on trips, they checked newsstands to see whether our magazine was displayed. We had, of course, a mutual agreement with the Soviet Government. We sold our *Amerika* and they sold their *Soviet Life* in the United States.

Now and then I had to visit Soyuzpechat to discuss matters of distribution. Those were always rather formal occasions, and never completely satisfying. There was the matter of Soviet censorship, and when the Soviets objected to material in our magazine, they would refuse to distribute it.

View from the Embassy balcony of the parade entering Red Square.

The Children's Centre Christmas Program, 1949: Erica is at far left, Randall is Santa, in the back row, and Mary is to his right. Maria is seated, and to her right are Ambassador Kirk and the British Ambassador, Sir David Kelly.

At first, their excuse was that people did not want to buy it, and "unsold" copies were returned to us. This situation developed into a collapse of the exchange agreement soon after I left Moscow in July 1951. Since then the agreement has been renewed, and *Amerika* and *Soviet Life* are still being published. [Publication of both magazines ended in 1991.]

While we were in Moscow, there were travel restrictions on all Embassy travel. We could move freely within a radius of 25 miles, or 40 kilometers, around Moscow.

There was a summer home in the country for the Ambassador; it was not used much as a residence, but mostly for picnics and parties. Our family was able to go to Zagorsk, an old monastery town of great charm. To go to Tolstoy's home at Yasnaya Polyana, and to Tchaikovsky's home, we only had to notify the Foreign Office beforehand.

To take other trips, we had to apply to Intourist for tickets. This required specific approval of the trip by the Soviet Foreign Office.

As Public Affairs Officer, I got to take more trips than any other Embassy officer except the Agricultural Attaché. I took a trip to the Ukraine (Odessa and Kharkov), to the Caucasus (Tbilisi) and to middle Siberia (Novosibirsk). I also made several trips to Leningrad.

Whenever I took such trips I was always followed by the Secret Police. I was never followed in Moscow, insofar as I was aware.

Америка

Amerika magazine was modeled on *Life* magazine and was filled with high-quality photographs and articles about Americans and how they lived.

Topics included sports, farming, science, industry, cars, fashion, and city and home life. Featured Americans ranged from artists and athletes such as Georgia O'Keefe (right) and Joe Lewis (below) to historical figures such as Ben Franklin and Thomas Jefferson.

After the articles and captions were written in New York and translated in Moscow, they were reviewed by Soviet censors; articles had to be timeless because censorship took anywhere from 10 days to 10 weeks.

Each issue was discussed by Russians and was widely shared, so that the magazine's circulation and impact greatly surpassed the number of copies sold.

Despite the fact that the Soviet officials returned many copies as unsold, long lines formed when *Amerika* went on sale. US officials felt that *Amerika* gave Soviet people a better understanding of our nation and that it countered Soviet propaganda about the West.

КАРТИНЫ ДЖОРДЖИИ О'КИФ

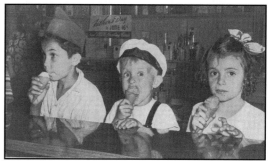

ДЖО ЛУИС, ЧЕМПИОН В ТЯЖЕЛОМ ВЕСЕ, ВЕРНУВШИСЬ

Dear Friends,

Moscow

Nov. 27, 1949

It has been a long time since some of you have heard from us and once again we are far from home. . . .Moscow is quite a busy metropolis with several impressive-looking buildings in the heart of the city near the Kremlin. The rest of the city is quite disheartening since there is no "nice" residential area but rather all slums with apartment houses and log houses all jammed together.

We are fortunate in that we live in a little house or "dacha" on the northern edge of the city. We have a lovely garden which is large enough so we can plant vegetables, have a lawn and still have room for the children to romp about freely. . .

The children are quite happy here and keep so busy that they have little time for boredom. At first when I was working at the Embassy, since all American wives must work, I taught the children in the afternoons. Now, however, since the Children's Centre for American and British children has been established and I have been made the director, the children go in to school with me every day.

Since there is no organized Protestant church here, we have our own worship service on Sunday mornings at home. We try to give the children an atmosphere as similar to that at "home" as possible. Living in a large city, however, has many advantages such as the museums, art galleries, theatres, and zoo. . . .

On my free afternoon I do the shopping since I have found from experience that I can do it more economically than the cook can. Prices for everything are high regardless of category. Compare these food prices with those you pay. Apples 50¢ apiece, lemons 63¢ apiece, eggs 22¢ apiece, beef $1.69 lb., pork even higher, bread 50¢ a kilo or 2.2 lbs., the cheapest cheese $2 lb., canned vegetables in glass $1.75 for #2 size but frozen peas and green beans are only 27¢ a pkg. and quite delicious. The glass jars make the canned goods more expensive. Fortunately we get the bulk of our supplies from our Commissary. But fresh foods come from the local markets.

Living in this country teaches us to love our homeland more than ever and to uphold and maintain her traditions. . . .

Love, Maria

Rynok, or farmers market.

In Russia we ate fried Spam, chicken chow mein with Chinese noodles, creamed chipped beef on toast, Welsh rarebit, and salami.

All these foods came out of cans from the States. Mother had ordered a two-year supply of food to be shipped to Moscow.

Our canned foods included early forms of dried milk and dried potatoes. Neither tasted like the real thing. We kids refused to drink the reconstituted dried milk, so Mother devised a milk soup with noodles. It became our primary source of milk, except for Russian ice cream, which was wonderful.

Erica

Paper bags are a great rarity in the Soviet Union, and when there are any, they are sold, not given away. Every shopper brings his own basket or string bag – even little aluminum pails if he wishes to buy milk. Only raw milk is sold in the Soviet Union, pasteurized milk being reserved for hospitals and mothers of newborn infants.

The housewives taste the milk by dipping their forefingers into the large bucket and licking them. In this way, a good housekeeper supposedly can tell not only the milk's quality but its fat content as well. It is not surprising that many Americans wait to go to Germany to drink milk.

Rev. Georges Bissonnette, US Chaplain in Moscow, 1953-55

There was a joke in our family for many years: How in the world do you figure out what to take for a two-year posting in Moscow? Answer: Take it all!

My mother did her very best. A few items have special significance for me, even after all these years:

1. Canned whole chickens. These Sunday Dinner Specials were presented with great ceremony (though they must have been pretty miserable eating).

2. Log Cabin syrup. It came in cans that looked like log cabins which became toys for me when empty.

3. Soap bars. Mom brought far more than we could use and was unable to sell off the remainder when we left Moscow. Perhaps everyone brought too much soap! We lugged it with us to Belgium and then on to Florence, finally using the last of it in 1957. Eight years of soap!

4. Powdered milk. Godawful, miserable stuff with foam on top. We hated it too. It will forever remind me of the bad old days in Moscow.

George Service

Produktovy magazin, or grocery store.

I remember very clearly accompanying our maid on trips to the local market and being followed by an obvious goon from the NKVD. Only later did I come to understand that his presence was intended to prevent Russians from engaging in any sort of contact with dangerous, subversive foreigners like me, age 7.

At the time it all seemed extremely strange though not particularly threatening. It was clearly understood in our own family that our Russian maid reported directly to the NKVD, keeping the secret service aware of what brand of toothpaste Dad used.

George Service

The Kremlin, a fortress city within a city, was built in the 1400s. Covering 90 acres, it sits in the heart of Moscow, overlooking the Moskva River.

The Kremlin was the Tsar's residence until 1712, when the court moved to St. Petersburg. Within the Kremlin walls are four palaces, four cathedrals and a bell tower. It now serves as the official residence of the President of Russia.

Stalin lived in this building inside the Kremlin walls.

Ralph said that he never expected to see Coca-Cola or other American brands sold in Moscow. This picture was taken by Erica in 2007.

Admiral Alan G. Kirk, above left, was commander of the US naval forces on D-Day, June 6, 1944. A career naval officer, he graduated from the Naval Academy in 1909, served in World War I, was Naval Attaché in London in 1939-1941, and commanded naval amphibious groups during the invasions of Sicily and Normandy. He retired from the Navy as a full admiral in 1946.

First posted to Belgium, he was US Ambassador to Moscow from 1949 to 1951. During that time, North Korea invaded South Korea, the Soviets blockaded Berlin, and the US and the USSR settled into the icy confrontation of the Cold War.

Embassy personnel never travelled alone. In Kharkov, in April 1951, we were always aware of the agent following us. He sat just behind us at the theater. When we were standing at a street corner where a streetcar stopped, a young man asked me where the streetcar went.

Before I could say I didn't know, the agent grabbed the fellow, shook him, and said, "How dare you talk to this foreigner!" It scared the fellow half out of his wits.

On the same trip, when we were ready to return to Moscow, we went into a telegraph office, wrote out a telegram to our Embassy, and presented it at the window. I was told that I would have to take it to the Central Post Office, which was in a part of the city we had been barred from entering.

With the telegram in hand, we attempted to get to the Central Post Office. We were stopped and were told to go to an office on the other side of the city. There I was told that I could send the telegram only at the Central Post Office.

When I told the lady we were not permitted to go there, she said, "I never heard of such as thing."

I said, "If you don't believe me, ask that fellow over there in the red tie."

That really embarrassed our follower. We returned to the center of the city, and this time we were allowed to go to the Central Post Office. I submitted the telegram with the agent looking over my shoulder!

Новосибирск Театр Оперы и Балета

Above: Opera house in Novosibirsk, considered at the time to be the finest modern opera house in the USSR.

Right: Railway terminal at Novosibirsk.

Новосибирск Вокзал

On a trip to Tbilisi, Georgia, we visited Stalin's home town and went up the Georgian Military Highway into the Caucasus Mountains. There is an old fortress, in ruins, in the city of Tbilisi (Tiflis). After climbing to the top, we found the sunshine so inviting that we stayed a while. Evidently a policeman got suspicious and conducted us off the hill and told us not to come back to that area.

My longest trip was to Novosibirsk, in Middle Siberia. It was in January and the weather was very cold – about 25° below zero.

We had reservations at a hotel. Assuming that we could get a taxi immediately to the hotel, we took our luggage outside the train station. There was no taxi, and the porter said he would go call us one. He didn't come back. We tried to get back into the railway station, but a fierce-looking guard would not let us in – only people who were taking a train could enter the station.

So we had to stand for more than three hours outside in the cold before a taxi finally came and took us to our hotel. Obviously we got very cold, but we were protected by our fur caps, fur-lined coats, and warm boots.

In Novosibirsk we had an unusual encounter. One evening the hotel dining-room was rather crowded, and we asked a lone gentleman if we could sit with him.

He turned out to be an Inspector for the Fisheries Ministry. He was on his way to Baku, to inspect the processing of caviar.

Passenger train schedule.

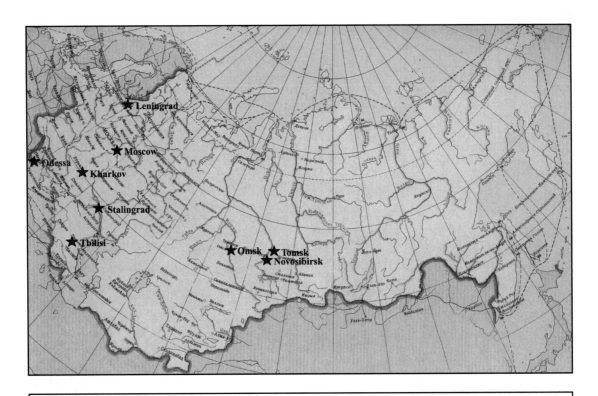

Ralph's destinations in 1951 as Public Affairs Officer.

January-February: Novosibirsk, Omsk, and Tomsk, all in middle Siberia.

April: Kharkov and Odessa, in Ukraine; and Stalingrad, in the Caucasus.

June: Tbilisi, in Georgia. July: Leningrad (now St. Petersburg, its original name).

When he found that we were Americans, he asked me whether I could get an American children's book for his young son who was in school. I was rather surprised at this request but I agreed to do it.

I asked him how I could get it to him after I received it from the States (where Maria and the children had returned for the birth of our youngest daughter). He told me to call a certain number in Moscow. Again I was puzzled, since we felt sure that all our telephone calls were monitored.

When the book arrived, I called the number and was told that the Inspector was not there. A few days later he called me, presumably from a public phone. I asked how I could get the book to him and he suggested meeting in Sokolniki Park.

I went to the Park, and after walking around a few minutes I saw him and gave him the book. I am still somewhat puzzled by the whole affair, but it shows how complicated a very innocent matter could become in the Soviet Union.

The cultural life in Moscow is very rich indeed. We took full advantage of our opportunities to go to the Bolshoi Theater for ballet and opera. There were children's theaters and the circus, both of which our children enjoyed. There were symphony concerts.

My special pleasure was attending theater performances at the Moscow Art Theater, the Maly, and half a dozen other theaters. Of course we saw a lot of Chekhov and Gorky, but my special love was the plays of Ostrovsky. The Canadian Minister and I shared this fascination with Ostrovsky, and we were always talking about the play we had just seen.

The site of our dacha had been part of Ostankino Palace grounds. We visited the Palace, built in the 1700s, and the children's town in Ostankino Park, where we ice skated on the pond, and rode the Ferris wheel and merry-go-round. While we lived in Moscow, the grounds were used for an Agricultural Exhibition.

Erica

Katok, or ice skating rink.

A Russian winter tale

Your home had a basement with a furnace. Our log cabin was equipped with a traditional Russian affair for warming the house.

In the center of our dacha was an extremely thick wall, inside of which was a space in which Dad built a fire. The heat radiated through the walls and quite effectively heated the central living areas, although the heat never seemed to reach the remote bedroom that my sister and I shared.

This "central heating system" required that Dad get up at least an hour before the rest of us so he could build up the fire and get some warmth into the house. One night he and Mother returned home from a very late affair and he thought he would simplify life by building an extra-large fire in the wall at 0200, hoping to be able to skip the usual 0400 stoking and get a bit of extra sleep.

The extra-large fire, however, ignited the insulation packed between the rafters (old newspapers) and brought the Russian fire department out in force.

We kids huddled out on the street, wrapped in blankets while the firemen ripped great holes in the roof in a very efficient manner. This was in January or February and it was colder than hell.

George Service

Dear Flo, Andy & children,

. . . .December was an exciting & thrilling month. It really started with Thanksgiving. We had just a family dinner – no guests – but turkey and all the trimmings. . . .

Moscow

Jan. 7, 1950

Temperature 22 degrees below 0

The next week we were included on a tour of the Kremlin. Every so often the Embassy can send 25 people on this tour. We took Erica – others will go in warmer weather. Ralph did the translating for the group.

We visited the outer grounds, looked at the wonderfully preserved mosaics on the very, very old churches. Then visited the museum, the big white Kremlin palace – look at the picture in the new Compton's (encyclopedia) – it's the long white building & is where the Council of the U.S.S.R. meets. . . .

In the museum we saw absolutely fabulous jewels & costumes weighted with jewels. Old church robes, court dress, etc. It was all fantastic to behold. The crown worn by Ivan, Boris, etc. Katherine's sleigh coach, her coronation gown, etc. It was a 2 1/2 hour tour & I shall try to go on another so as to be able to absorb more of it.

The Palaces – especially the old ones – were fascinating with their decorative walls, windows and porcelain stoves. We were greeted at the gate by two men in uniform and later joined by a lady guide and another man. They kept us all together and a few times when I lagged behind I was told politely in Russian I must stay with the group.

Two nights afterwards Amb. & Mrs. Kirk asked Ralph & me around for an early dinner and then the opera. It was just a family affair, and since I was late to begin with – the children and I had been to the British Ambassadress Lady Kelly's tea and Xmas party and I had to send the children home with the chauffeur – we rushed thru dinner, hopped into the Amb.'s car & off we went to the opera.

As we got out of the car two Russian civilians moved up very close to us. I started, but the Amb. grabbed my arm and said, "Don't be afraid, Maria, that's just the 'boys'." I'd completely forgotten about his Russian 'body guards' who accompany him everywhere and follow him in a black Plymouth. Protection so they say.

Well, back to the opera. We saw "Boris Godunov" and some of the costumes were authentic ones like we had seen only a couple days before in the Kremlin. It was the most splendid production I have ever seen and excellently sung. Then to top it off, the Amb. sent us home in his car which is a long, low-slung job!!!

I'm still trying to figure out the why & wherefore of the whole evening & have come to the only conclusion – they like us. Both the Amb. & Mrs. Kirk are so sweet & friendly that you feel immediately at home with them.

Oh yes – style note – that night I wore my taffeta suit with the bow in back – Martha will remember. I'm so glad I did my shopping in Maryville last Spring.

After that I settled down to preparing for our big Xmas party to which we invited about 140-150 guests. I worried about having the children present, thinking they'd get tired & irritable and had made arrangements with some of the single men to sort of take them in tow.

But my fears were groundless – Randall singled out certain people he wanted to talk to, especially the Canadian Air Attaché whose last name is Randall & several of our Western men, so he had a grand time.

The girls looked sweet in twin yellow dresses and they plied the guests with canapés & cookies to the point where many told me afterwards they'd never eaten so much at a party before. Well, at least there was plenty to go around. And if the children didn't make the party informal, the long ride – 1/2 hour – to our "dacha" did – because by the time people got here all reserve had disappeared & everyone was very natural.

I had a lighted Xmas tree in front of the house & if that alone wasn't enough to attract the Russians from nearby, then the parade of cars was. I missed the outside show, but they say two Russian police came in a hurry to direct traffic. I'm sorry I missed that....

About 16 stayed for supper and carols – and I'm convinced more than ever that people like to be natural and have a good time!! Oh yes – I wore my olive-green dress – MacArthur's -- & red slippers. Randall said I looked like a "Xmas tree"!!

The following Friday I had my program at school and the preparations were more nerve-wracking than the actual performance. Both British and American Ambassadors accepted my invitation and came with their wives. Both Ambassadors spoke and posed for pictures with the children & Santa.

Needless to say the children were darling and everything went beautifully. Randall chastised Santa for spelling his name wrong on his gift which sent the audience into a fit of laughter, since Randall was still in his Santa costume from the play. Yes, I had to make a Santa costume – used Russian flag material and yards of surgical cotton!

Then Xmas eve I started preparing for our own Xmas. The chauffeur and I toured the market and I finally found a goose – Randall's idea of a real Xmas bird. With much scurrying around I got the tree up and it looked lovely. I bought some Russian decorations which they use for their New Year's trees.

After the stockings were hung and the children in bed, Ralph & I went to the Ambassador's Xmas Eve Buffet and carol sing. Only Americans were there so it was very home-like. Everyone left early either to go to the Catholic Midnight Mass or home.

Very early Xmas morning the children were up to see what Santa had left – they all still believe – altho they realize he is only a Spirit – but nonetheless he is very real to them. Fortunately, the last of our Xmas packages arrived on Xmas Eve so we had a very elaborate Xmas. Cowboy & cowgirl outfits were our main interest altho books especially on American folklore and Greek mythology seemed to please the children very much.

Later Xmas a.m. we went to a church service conducted by a minister from the Church of England in Helsinki, Finland. It was a lovely service altho different from ours, and was well attended by both British & Americans. After Xmas there was a succession of parties for both children and adults.

New Year's Eve there was a dance at the Ambassador's to which the whole diplomatic colony had been invited. Since there were official guests to be greeted, I kept busy shaking hands up 'til midnight – after that everybody relaxed and enjoyed the buffet and dancing.

Fashion note – I wore my oldest evening gown – that old white satin-back crepe and my sequin jacket Ralph bought for me in Miller's. And you should have heard the compliments. I enjoy nothing better than to take the wind out of some officious gal's sails when she tries to be so goo-gooey about your clothes, and I say, "Oh yes—this is strictly American – I bought it in Tennessee"!!

. . . .It has been rather cold this week – 22 to 27 degrees below zero. But it's so dry & clear that if you're warmly dressed it's quite invigorating. The children now have fur hats and fur liners for their coats. Mother had my furrier in New York make them up and they got here just before the cold set in.

But it's now too cold for them to stay out more than 10 minutes to play without getting frostbite. We're making a skating rink in our garden. We have only a little snow so far but I'm sure more will come as it warms up.

We think of you all so often. . . .Give my best to all the girls – tell them they are so lucky to have such a wonderful way of life and beautiful homes and fine families. I pray none of us will become lax in our efforts to preserve our American way of life. These people here are working and striving to achieve their aims and it's quite evident all about but they still have such a long way to go. Just don't let us sit on our laurels. We must strive too.

Love to you all and Happy New Year.

. . . .For last two weeks pipes froze, toilet froze, furnace pipes burst, so children and I have been making 1 & 2 night stopovers with friends who have room to put a couple of us up here and there. It has been a long aggravating situation with inadequate supplies to make repairs, etc. Tonight we are trying it at home altho only two rooms are heated. Plumbing is finally back in order. Children are holding up well but getting tired of being carted around. . . .

Jan. 22, 1950

Love, Maria

Embassy children attended summer camp at the dacha. Mary Johanna in center.

Below: the dacha is beyond to the left and the street is to the right. The garage is in the center background, and the root cellar roof is seen at far right.

During the summer the school's playground equipment was moved to the dacha.

Mother wanted playground equipment for the new school for Embassy children. She wrote to an Army officer she knew in Berlin and arranged to have pipes shipped to Moscow to build a jungle gym and a swing set.

The equipment was set up in the front yard of the school, which was in a large house on Ulitsa Kalinina (now Novi Arbat). When we children played outside, the Russians passing by stopped and peered through the metal fence to watch us until the Russian militia guard on duty chased them away.

Erica

For her son Arturo's birthday party, Hilda set up a table in front of the garage where she and her children lived. Arturo is at the head of the table with Mary Johanna to his right. Erica is second from the right and Randall is fourth from the right. The other children lived in the neighborhood.

We had almost no social life with the Russians. Unless they were officials, they were afraid to associate with Westerners. Even at the official functions at our Ambassador's residence, only a few officials from the Soviet Foreign Office attended, and for only about a half-hour.

This lack of social contact with Russians probably intensified the social activities among the Western Embassy personnel. We were constantly being invited to Italian, French, British, Swedish, Lebanese, Finnish, and other Embassy parties. The first year, 1949-50, they tended to elaborate formality, but the second year the parties were less formal.

Although Embassy personnel predominated, the social scene involved all Westerners, including news correspondents and fur traders. Among the American correspondents were Harrison Salisbury, Tom Whitney, Ed Stephens, and Eddy Gilmore. Tom and Eddy had Russian wives, who were lively additions to our social occasions.

Some of the trips related above were taken after Maria and the children left Moscow in August 1950. They sailed from Leningrad and I accompanied them as far as Bergen, Norway. We had stopovers in Helsinki and Stockholm, and we spent almost a week in Oslo, staying at the Vettakollen, on the way up to the famous ski-slope of Holmenkollen.

As Maria and the children left Bergen on the Norwegian ship *Oslofjord* to cross the Atlantic, I took the train from Bergen back to Oslo and on to Copenhagen. After a few days there I went on to Germany for a vacation.

Above: the side of the dacha, showing the vegetable garden and other plantings and the third floor where food and other supplies were stored.

Right: high-rise apartment buildings now occupy the spot where the dacha stood.

Maria and the children returned to Cornwall-on Hudson, where Melissa was born on October 27.

From Berlin I flew back to Moscow on the Ambassador's plane, taking along a crate of celery – unknown and unavailable in Moscow – to distribute to all the American Embassy families.

Back in Moscow I lived with several Embassy bachelors at an old town-house on Vesnina Street. The dacha we had lived in had been the property of a Russian lady-doctor who lived in Switzerland and who died about the time my family returned to the States, so the Embassy released the dacha to the municipality of Moscow, which made it available to Russians needing housing.

In the spring of 1951, I went out to Ostankino and walked past the house. A woman was working in the garden, and I spoke to her. She said 18 adult Russians were living in the house, six of them in the attic. As we had considered the house quite small for two adults and three children, you can get an idea of the severe shortage of housing for Russians in Moscow in those days.

The Americans who served at our Embassy during those two years shared an experience which has remained a tight bond among us. From Admiral and Mrs. Kirk to the lowly third secretaries, we were a group deeply devoted to our jobs and bound together by both troubles and joys.

We were known as the Embassy generation who expressed their joys and troubles in song. Who among us will ever forget our song "Skoro budet" and many others?

View from Ralph's apartment at 16 Vesnina.

The Cold War crisis: 1949-1950

Ralph's assignment in Moscow took place at a crucial phase in the escalation of Cold War hostilities between the US and the Soviets and their Communist allies.

In June 1949, Mao's Communist forces took power to establish the People's Republic of China, and Chiang Kai-shek's Nationalist forces retreated to the island of Formosa (now known as Taiwan). The world-wide Communist revolution had won its second major success and appeared to be spreading.

Moreover, the USSR was visibly expanding its military power. In September 1949, US intelligence learned that the Soviets had exploded an atomic bomb, effectively ending the monopoly on nuclear weapons that the US had held since 1945. The atomic arms race had begun.

In June 1950 the Korean War began, as Communist North Korea attacked South Korea. By August, US and Korean forces had been pushed back to a small perimeter in the extreme south. In September 1950, US forces based in Japan carried out an amphibious landing behind North Korean lines at Inchon and advanced into the north. As the US forces approached the Chinese border in October, Chinese troops counter-attacked from Manchuria.

By January 1951, the two sides had settled down to a battlefront at the 38th parallel, roughly where the border between North and South Korea had been when the war began. In 1952 Dwight Eisenhower campaigned for President with a promise to end the conflict. A cease-fire was established in July 1953.

Thus the period when Ralph Collins was in Moscow, July 1949 to July 1951, was at the lowest point of American-Soviet relations. A special concern of the State Department was whether the USSR would enter the Korean War on the side of North Korea and China, and how much military aid it was giving.

Because the Soviets had atomic weapons, the possibility of using nuclear weapons against China, as Gen. Douglas MacArthur, the US commander in the Far East, suggested in 1950, might escalate into full-scale nuclear war.

This was part of the reason President Truman fired MacArthur in 1951. President Eisenhower, on the other hand, secretly threatened the Communists with using nuclear weapons if they did not sign the Armistice in 1953 – which they did.

I had little sense of all of these developments, being 8 years old when the Korean War broke out. I saw the front page of the *Stars and Stripes*, the US military newspaper, which was available at the embassy, with its maps of the military forces sweeping up and down the Korean peninsula.

It was clear that there was a lot of anti-American hostility in Moscow. Posters on walls depicted Uncle Sam and General MacArthur as ferocious war-mongers, and depicted America as loaded with chains representing capitalism.

Little Russian boys threw rocks over our gate at the dacha, presumably because they heard that some of the American enemies lived there. Being 8 years old, I did not find this frightening but rather exciting.

With all the sophistication of childhood, I hoped that the war would go on long enough so that I could grow up and take part in it. Perhaps around this time came my career ambition to be an army officer, an ambition which my Grandfather Alfred Zubiller encouraged and which lasted until my mid-teens.

Randall Collins

It was all flat on paper, but they forgot about the ravines and have to make their way over them!

General MacArthur and a South Korean ally study a map of the Korean peninsula.

Above and lower right: Yasnaya Polyana, "Bright Glade," where Count Tolstoy was born, lived, and is buried.

Lower left: Tolstoy on his farm on the estate.

Among the group were such solid Foreign Service Officers as Wally Barbour (later Ambassador to Israel), Ray Thurston (later Ambassador in Mogadisciu), Dick Service, Scott Lyon, Charles Stefan, Robert Blake, Culver Greysteen, John Keppel, and James Pratt. The last was an especially close friend, and his wife, Vaughn, was my secretary when I was Public Affairs Officer.

My departure from Moscow was preceded by a strange occurrence. On a Sunday in the latter part of June 1951, I accompanied a small group of Embassy personnel to Yasnaya Polyana, Tolstoy's home. We visited the home, the grave, and the museum.

The Director of the Museum took us through personally, showing us some of the items of especial interest to Americans, such as one of Edison's model phonographs and a portrait of William Jennings Bryan.

At the end of the Museum visit, we decided to write a word of appreciation in the visitors' book. I wrote it, in Russian, and we all signed it. We were then ready to leave, but another group of younger people from our Embassy arrived at that time. One of them asked me to find out what a Russian, who had followed him from the parking lot, was asking.

I spoke to the Russian, who asked something about holidays for young people in the US. As I answered him, I was surrounded by several hundred Russians who wanted to ask questions. I knew that I should leave, and as I was looking for the best way out, a policeman came to me and led me out of the crowd. We left and returned to Moscow.

Tolstoy, a novelist and moral philosopher, best known for *War and Peace* and *Anna Karenina*, was also an early champion of nonviolent protest and was influential in the social restlessness that swept Russia before the 1917 revolution.

Gorky, a novelist and playwright, used his friendship with Lenin and his post as head of the state publishing house to aid writers and artists. He is considered the father of Soviet literature and founder of the doctrine of Socialist Realism which was proclaimed by the Union of Soviet Writers as compulsory practice in 1932.

Leo Tolstoy and Maxim Gorky at Yasnaya Polyana in 1900.

The following Thursday the newspaper *Literaturnaya Gazeta* carried a front-page article entitled "Savages at Yasnaya Polyana." It said that a group of US Embassy people had desecrated the tomb of Tolstoy by their loud and boisterous behavior, and that the ring-leaders were Ralph Collins and Norman Stines.

It went on to say that we were so ashamed of our conduct that we didn't dare put our names in the visitors' book. I had reported what had happened to the Embassy and the Department on the previous Monday. I thought I was most certainly going to be declared persona non grata.

In the end, I was not, but I departed promptly a week or so later, on the exact date of finishing my two-year assignment in Moscow. On Sunday, 24 June 1951, *The New York Times* carried an account on page 1 of the Yasanaya Polyana incident, by Harrison Salisbury: "Russians say U.S. Embassy Aides Desecrated the Grave of Tolstoy".

When I left Moscow in July, I had orders for home leave and transfer to Regensburg, Germany, to attend Detachment-R, the Army Advanced Russian Training post. I again had stop-overs in Helsinki and Stockholm, then went by train to Paris, where I made a point of eating at the Pommier Normand, a place I knew from 1932-33, near Place de l'Odéon. I crossed the Atlantic on the *Île-de-France*, travelling with Wally Barbour. It was a deluxe trip, which brought me back to my family and my new daughter, Melissa.

The New York Times

Russians Say U. S. Embassy Aides Desecrated the Grave of Tolstoy

By HARRISON E. SALISBURY
Special to The New York Times.

MOSCOW, June 23—Under the headline "Savages in Yasnaya Polyana," the Literary Gazette charged today that a group of ten United States Embassy staff members had desecrated the grave of Leo Tolstoy by boisterous, drunken and improper behavior.

An investigation of the charges by the newspaper was quickly made by the embassy at the direction of the United States Ambassador, Admiral Alan G. Kirk, who has himself on several occasions visited the home and the grave of the classic Russian writer situated about 120 miles south of Moscow.

The embassy issued a formal statement declaring:

"The American Embassy states with reference to the article published this morning in the Literary Gazette, which charges various members of the embassy with improper conduct at Yasnaya Polyana on June 10, that Americans, including members of the embassy, have of course, the highest respect for Tolstoy and his works and that upon investigation it appears that any impression to the contrary that may have been given on the occasion in question was seemingly due to a misunderstanding arising from language difficulties."

The Literary Gazette article compared the conduct of the Americans to that of Germans during the war. When the Germans occupied Yasnaya Polyana in 1941 they tore up the ground around Tolstoy's grave to bury their own dead, cut down a number of trees around the grave and ravaged the building that had been Tolstoy's

Continued on Page 31, Column 2

Front page article in *The New York Times*, Sunday, June 24, 1951.

RUSSIANS ACCUSE 10 IN U. S. EMBASSY

Continued From Page 1

home, starting fires in several rooms of the house.

Tolstoy's home is now a state museum and is one of the favorite excursion points of the diplomatic corps, including the American Embassy staff. It is the longest automobile trip that the diplomats may make from Moscow without special dispensation.

The Literary Gazette charged that the Americans appeared at Tolstoy's home under the influence of liquor and that they shouted and yelled and jostled Soviet visitors in the Tolstoy house.

The Literary Gazette said the Americans laughed uproariously and made loud and rude remarks about everything they saw and "demonstratively expressed contempt for the place where they were and the people who created and care for this museum of world significance."

"With assertive tones, with rudeness and with their entire behavior, and particularly with hostile attacks, they clearly tried to provoke into rudeness or sharp retorts Soviet people in the park," the paper said. "But they were met with nothing but controlled calmness and deadly answers."

The Literary Gazette listed the names of eight Americans at Yasnaya. The senior American Embassy officials present in the party were First Secretary Norman Stines and Second Secretary Ralph Collins.

This is the first occasion in many months in which the Soviet press has attacked the conduct of the American Embassy personnel in Moscow.

Others Listed in Party

MOSCOW, June 23 (AP)—The Literary Gazette said the embassy's First Secretary Norman Stines and Second Secretary Ralph Collins acted as guides for the group. The last names listed as other members of the party were Good, Forman, Branaman and Long.

These apparently referred to Yeoman First Class Walter Good of the United States naval attaché's office; Chief Pharmacist's Mate Charles Forman of Gadsden, Ala., president of the American House Club in Moscow; Jacqueline Branaman, secretary - archivist from Brownstown, Ind., and either Chief Warrant Officer John Long of the United States military attaché's office or his wife.

[Others named, according to The United Press, were Paul John Dell, an aide of a military or naval attaché, and Priscilla Handy, an embassy stenographer.]

Regensburg, with Gumpelsheimerstrasse in upper left, parallel to the Danube River.

Germany

1951-1954

Assignment: Germany

We had a very enjoyable summer together in New York, and visited in Washington and North Carolina. The three older children had to attend three different schools during the 1951-52 school year.

They started school in Cornwall-on-Hudson for about a month, then we went to Regensburg, where they attended an American school for military and government dependents. After six months there, they finished the year in Frankfurt.

They coped with that situation very nicely, as a matter of fact. I don't see that their constant change of schools through high school did them any harm. On the contrary, it was an enriching experience. Melissa learned German first, because she was not yet 1 year old when we arrived in Regensburg, and our housekeeper talked to her constantly in German.

We left New York City October 16, 1951, and travelled on the *Nieuw Amsterdam*. We landed in Rotterdam and drove through Holland to Germany, to Regensburg, on the Danube River in Bavaria. Our house was waiting for us, at Gumpelsheimerstrasse 12. It was good-sized and comfortable, with good yard space for the children to play in.

Detachment R (Det R) was set up by the US Army after World War II for advanced training in the Russian language for selected officers. At the time I attended, it was in Regensburg. It was later moved to Oberammergau, where I think it is still in operation.

Above: Easter 1952. Below: Melissa, 9 months; Mary Johanna, 8½; Randall, 10; and Erica, 11.

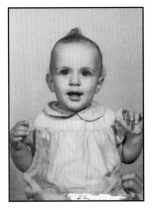

When I attended, the instructors, or professors, were various displaced Russians and others. I recall the names of some of the faculty: Osipov, from Leningrad; Krylov, and Grigorich, all Russian; Bozich, a Yugoslav; and Kunta, from the Caucasus. Later, when Grigorich was in Washington, we saw him many times, especially for a Russian Christmas – always a very jolly affair with lots of food and good cheer.

In 1951-52 Jim Pratt and I were the only State Department, or rather, Foreign Service Officers, attending Det R. Among the Army students were Col. Charles Timmes, Ted Tansey, Flip Corcoran, Seymour, and Kravitz. Lt. Colonel Al Martin was in charge of Det R, assisted by Major Charles Whitmire.

It was a fine group of officers and we had a good time with them. Our main exercise was bowling. There were other military in Regensburg, so there were many facilities, including a Dependent's School. One week, when we were in Oberammergau for some special military classes, Jim Pratt and I took one day off to go up the Zugspitze, the highest peak in the Bavarian Alps.

We took the family and Jim on a trip to Vienna, but Maria became ill and had to return home by train, and our daughter Mary accompanied her. The rest of us returned by car.

At Thanksgiving, Jim and I went in his English car on a trip to Switzerland. We covered some of the same places I had visited in 1932. We took other trips by boat along the Danube, which is very pretty around Regensburg, especially going upstream to Straubing.

Jim Pratt and his English car in a typical German countryside setting.

Left to right: Ralph, Vaughn and Jim Pratt, Maria, and medical student Hermann Hofmann.

Maria and I, who had the best command of German, developed quite a few friendships with the German society of Regensburg. Herr Doktor Schmidt recommended a piano teacher for Erica. We attended many musical events, including one where Karl Schmidt-Walter sang. He and his wife were surprised to see us, as we had not seen each other since 1948 in Berlin.

Through a Professor at the Medical School in Regensburg, Dr. Anton Kiesler, we met a lot of students, some of whom we later saw at Würzburg. One of them, Dr. Paul Tueffers, from East Germany, is now a physician in Seattle. We had great fun with the students and attended several of their Fasching (Carnival) balls.

When we moved to Bad Homburg, near Frankfurt, the following April, we kept up some of our friendships made in Regensburg, and had the pleasure of seeing our friends in our home in Bad Homburg and again in Regensburg, which we had occasion to revisit. We loved the city, its people, the Cathedral and many historic spots.

Bad Homburg was originally a resort town, with mineral springs and baths. It became a suburb of Frankfurt am Main and had many fine homes.

Our house, at Quellenweg 2, was nice and large, with a full basement and three floors above. We had plenty of bedrooms on the second floor, and several more on the top floor for guests. From the front of the house we looked across at the Kur-park, not far from the Chinese pavilion.

Top left: a view of the house, with Randy on fence. Above right: Visit by Lisa, Auguste, and Richard Zubiller. Below left: the family's 1952 Christmas portrait. Below right: another view of the house.

The PTA Council in Frankfurt am Main in 1953-54, when Maria, seated center, was president.

Dear Flo, Andy and children

Bad Homburg

July 31, 1952

. . . The house is very large and since I have only one woman to help me, I keep busy just trying to run things evenly. The garden was a wilderness when we came and only by hiring a man and Ralph and the children helping have we been able to get it in order. The fruit trees – cherry, plum, pear and apple – are all full and I have been able to make some jam. . . .

Bad Homburg

Sept. 2, 1952

. . . .We have had almost a continual round of guests because Frankfurt is a central place and people are always passing thru. . . . the surrounding territory offers such historical sites as a restored Roman Camp and fort, the remains of the palace of Frederick Barbarosa (Red Beard), the birthplace of the Grimm brothers, and almost everywhere are old castles or ruins thereof sitting on top of hills or mountain tops all of which tell tales of long, long ago. . . There is really much to see and do here. . . .

On a wall in Missy's room, I put the alphabet picture you made for Erica so long ago. The letters and pictures have withstood many washings and with a bit of crayon look quite new again. The only hitch, as the children pointed out, is how can Missy learn the alphabet and pictures when she knows only German. . . .

Ralph bought us a very nice ping-pong table recently. It folds so it can be moved around with us. We have set it up in a big room on the first floor and most of our spare time is now spent batting the little white ball around. . . .

Bad Homburg

Xmas Letter

. . . .Our house is large and very comfortably furnished. Below the terrace at the front of the house, there is a lovely formal rose garden and in the back there is an extensive garden with many berry bushes and fruit trees, all of which have yielded us a good harvest. In the center is a round space enclosed by tall evergreens. Randall built us a small fireplace there and all summer long that is where we held our picnics. Several times we had German guests and our typical wiener-marshmallow roast was such a novelty to them that even a sudden shower which drove the rest of us indoors could not dampen their spirits. . . . .

. . . .Last week we moved into a big 4-bedroom apartment in the HICOG [High Command – Germany] project. Everything is wonderfully modern and there's even an automatic Bendix [washing machine] and a drying room in the basement. . . . Although we shall miss our big garden in Bad Homburg, it's much more convenient here since we are within walking distance of school, dispensary, PX, other stores. . . .

Frankfurt a.M.
Nov. 30, 1952

. . . .Yesterday I took Erica, Randall and Mary sledding at the old Roman Camp at Saalburg. . . the setting deep among the trees was quite charming. The old Roman road runs parallel to the main highway but is deeper into the woods and so makes a wonderfully long ride which is quite safe for the children. They were intrigued by the thought that over 1500 years ago, Roman occupation children had probably gone sledding on that very road.

Frankfurt a.M.
Jan. 12, 1953

As always on Sundays, hundreds of Germans were out driving and walking. It's traditional that Sunday is excursion day and everyone who is able gets out of the house and goes somewhere even if it's only for a walk around the city. Then too it is customary to stop at a café, which you find deep in the woods or any place else where people might wander to, and have coffee and cake. . . . And what cakes – rich and gooey with buttercream frostings or whipped cream. The children and I went into the café at Saalburg to have hot chocolate and it was really quite delicious. . . .

. . . .I've been sewing like mad all summer trying to keep the children and myself in clothes. I'm having Erica a coat made in Grey fleece [out of] a piece of material I've been carrying around for years. Cheaper than buying one. . . .

Frankfurt a.M.
Aug. 30, 1953

All resorts or spas (and every little place that can boast mineral springs or just plain good fresh air or lots of sunshine is a spa) try to offer their summer guests or tourists some sort of entertainment, and music by real live musicians is the chief form. That's one thing that's so nice here, everywhere there are little and big orchestras playing for listening and dancing pleasure. Only when we go into American installations do we get back to canned music. . . .

Love, Maria

Clockwise from top left: Melissa in sandbox at HICOG Project, where the family lived in Frankfurt; Melissa's second birthday, October 1952; Erica with her piano teacher, Frau Emma Lübbecke-Job; and Erica with Taffy.

Our office was in Frankfurt, in the I.G. Farben building. My job was a specialized one – interrogating Soviet defectors as to their social background, their experiences, their motivation for defecting, and so on.

The subjects of our interrogation were in the town of Ober-Ursel, and we went there to interrogate them. (In the strawberry season, I stopped at the strawberry fields to buy freshly picked berries, of the same rich quality as those being flown from there to Paris.)

Our Frankfurt unit was technically part of our Embassy in Bonn, but we seldom had any necessity to go to Bonn, as we received our pay, etc. in Frankfurt. There was a fairly large Consulate General in Frankfurt, but most of the officers there seemed to think that we were working for the CIA, and they did not have social contact with us. Of course, CIA officers were also interrogating defectors, and we knew some of them fairly well.

Walter Stoessel was our chief officer for part of the first year, and then his place was taken by Charles Stefan, whom I knew very well from Moscow. Among the other officers in our group were Tom Donovan, Dick Johnson, Jack Shaw, Ralph Jones, and Stan Prisbeck. We also had many friends among the US military officers.

In November 1952 we moved into a roomy apartment in the HICOG project in Frankfurt. The schools for American children were excellent, and our three older children liked Frankfurt very much. Maria was President of the Frankfurt PTA one year.

Melissa on hood of the family Ford.

Clockwise from top left: Ralph with Mary Johanna and Melissa at Neuschwanstein; Erica overlooking Neuschwanstein Castle; Randall with his godmother, Mary Gladys Pieper (left), on a Rhine river cruise on his birthday; Maria and Mary Johanna waiting for the bus taking her to summer camp.

The family went on holiday to Sylt on the North Sea. The house with thatched roof, built in 1769, was modern inside. Right: Randall at Boy Scout camp in the Bavarian Alps.

The Collins family in the courtyard of the Zubiller home in Dörnbach, Rheinpfalz, 1954.

Randall was active in the Boy Scouts. All three older children went to the summer camps for American children, spending one summer at Füssen down in the lake and Alps area.

Again we had many new friends in the German community. Erica had a wonderful piano teacher, Frau Emma Lübbecke-Job, whose husband was a well-known Frankfurt historian, and his 1952 book on the history of Frankfurt is among my prized possessions. Frau Hellbusch-Tomascheck, a fine artist, painted pastel portraits of our four children. We took full advantage of the Frankfurt theaters and opera.

We had a good opportunity to get acquainted with all of Maria's kinfolk in the Rheinpfalz. We visited them and they visited us. Some of the medical students in Regensburg had moved to the University of Würzburg. They not only visited us but invited us to a rousing student banquet and celebration in Würzburg. In the summer of 1953 we spent a vacation at the beach on the island of Sylt, up near Denmark.

In February 1954 I received orders transferring me to Belgrade, Yugoslavia. I was disappointed when the transfer was cancelled, and I was returned to the State Department in Washington as Public Affairs Adviser in the Office of Eastern European Affairs.

Downtown Washington DC, up to the National Zoo.

Washington DC
1954-1957

Two views of the house on Woodley Place, a block from Connecticut Avenue, near Calvert Street Bridge, with Melissa on sidewalk at right in 1955, and Erica on steps at left in 2007.

Assignment: Washington

In my assignment in Washington, I followed my colleague and close friend, Jim Pratt. In April 1952 I had been promoted to FSO-4, and in February 1956 I was promoted to FSO-3.

In my job as Public Affairs Adviser, I dealt with representatives of the press and of public organizations with respect to American policy on East European questions. During the Krushchev-Matzkevich period, I was quite busy with both of these groups.

I attended a lot of lunches at the Washington Press Club. I also contributed to the Secretary of State's briefing book for his regular conferences.

As it was John Foster Dulles' term as Secretary of State and because he considered himself the supreme expert on Soviet and East European affairs, I doubt that he ever paid any attention to my suggestions as to how to answer questions from the Press.

However, I did write a speech for the Director of the Office of Eastern European Affairs, Ray Thurston, who was a good friend in Moscow and who later became an Ambassador to Mogadisciu.

In 1955 I got to take a trip to Eastern Europe. From June 28 to July 27 I visited all the EE countries except Bulgaria. In Moscow I saw Khrushchev at the Fourth of July party at the US embassy.

The Collins family (right) – Ralph, Maria, Linda Toepert (Maria's cousin), and Erica – see Jim and Vaughn Pratt off as they sail from New York to Europe. Below: Ralph, far right, and colleagues in the Consular Training Class, 1957.

Clockwise from top left: Randall and Melissa; Melissa at the National Zoo, a block from the Collins' home; Mary Johanna and Maria; Melissa and Ralph.

McCarthyism and the State Department

Ralph's time in the State Department in the late 1940s and early 50s was a period when the Department was under vicious attack by political opponents in the US. After the fall of China to the Communists in 1949, conservative Republicans began a campaign to pin the blame on "who lost China."

In February 1950, Senator Joseph McCarthy of Wisconsin made a speech to the Republican Women's Club in Wheeling, West Virginia, in which he said: "I have here in my hand a list of 205 – a list of names that were made known to the Secretary of State as being members of the Communist Party and who nevertheless are still working and shaping policy in the State Department." McCarthy later revised the number of communists downward to 57 or 81; in fact he had only some internal investigative reports which had the names blanked out. McCarthy went on to accuse President Truman and the Democrats of being soft on Communism, and he called the Roosevelt and Truman administrations "twenty years of treason."

When Eisenhower took office in 1953, Senator McCarthy chaired a Senate Permanent Subcommittee on Investigations, which attacked many officials of the Federal government. The State Department took the brunt of the first attacks, as McCarthy's committee accused the Voice of America and the United States Information Agency (USIA) of being full of communist employees.

It should be noted that Ralph Collins worked directly with the USIA in his duties in Moscow in 1949-51, in effect running the Moscow branch of the office at the Embassy. But he was not personally attacked by McCarthy. To his family, Ralph spoke little openly about McCarthy and the anti-communist investigations.

Although he was a liberal Democrat and a supporter of the Roosevelt New Deal, Ralph was not a politically partisan person. He expressly regarded his job as a Foreign Service Officer as representing the American government and people as a whole, not a particular party. In fact, our family conversation was so non-partisan that I scarcely knew the difference between Democrats and Republicans until I went to college at Harvard in 1959.

It was clear, though, that Ralph did not much care for the Republican administration of the State Department in the 1950s, under Eisenhower's Secy. of State, John Foster Dulles. Dulles had defended the State Department against McCarthy's charges, but in a tepid way in his public statements. Dulles himself made hard-line anti-communist speeches throughout his administration. From hints dropped by Ralph and Maria Collins in family conversations, it was apparent that Ralph thought Dulles was vindictive against Foreign Service Officers who did not share his line; they would not necessarily be fired but might be sent to an undesired post like Iceland or the Arabian desert. This was no doubt another reason to be non-partisan and keep one's mouth shut about one's own political position during the 1950s.

Ralph did remark to me later that he often was called in to brief Secretary Dulles before his speeches. Ralph was an acknowledged expert on Communism, and a Russian-language expert with first-hand experience travelling widely in the Soviet Union, a closed territory for most people. Ralph jokingly told me, during his retirement, that "Communism made my career." Since his superiors were so interested in Communism, he made it a point with every new assignment to work up a report on the history of the local communist party. This always got him a commendation from superiors, and no doubt the calls to brief the Secretary of State, even if Ralph personally did not like him.

Senator McCarthy fell from public acclaim in 1954, after he began to attack the Army for similar treasonous influences. In December 1954, McCarthy was censored by the US Senate. But the anti-communist crusade continued to have a strong influence throughout the 1950s, and into the early Kennedy administration in 1961. Ralph's transfer to Latin America in 1960 was part of a policy to send communist experts to combat the spread of communist revolutions there, just as they were spreading in the de-colonization period taking place in Asia, Africa and elsewhere in the world.

Nevertheless, Ralph's attitude was a pragmatic one; he believed in reaching out to make contacts with people on the other side wherever possible. In this respect he was very much the diplomat. As he once told me about diplomatic negotiations with enemy forces: "As long as they keep talking with each other, it's better than killing each other."

Randall Collins

Ralph and Maria at a reception at the Soviet embassy in Washington DC.

I then visited Warsaw, Berlin, Prague, Vienna, Budapest, and Belgrade. I was unable to visit Sofia, as it was temporarily without a US Ambassador. Of course, Albania was out, too.

While in Washington, we lived in a rented house at 2753 Woodley Place, NW. It was so close to the National Zoo that we sometimes heard a lion roar at night.

Erica attended Western High School in Georgetown, graduating in 1957. Among other things, she was editor of the school year-book and valedictorian of her class.

Randall went to Gordon Junior High and had a year at Western. As a Scout, he went on a trip to Philmont, New Mexico.

Mary went first to Oyster Elementary and then to Gordon. Melissa attended Kindergarten and made great gains in her fluency in speaking English.

In Washington, we saw many of our friends and associates as they came and went on assignment or home leave. There were the Freers, Donovans, Reveys, Sockoloskis, Kravitz, Woods, Horners, Reeds, Krylov, Roberts, Defranceski, and Stefans.

We got to know a couple from the Japanese Embassy, the Takahashis, and we had several occasions to visit the Soviet Embassy.

Central Bilbao.

View from apartment in Algorta with a view of the Bay of Biscay and San Ignacio Church.

Assignment: Bilbao

Early in 1957, I learned that I was to be assigned as Consul and Principal Officer in Bilbao, Spain. Erica was graduating from high school and was going to study at the University of Rochester and the Eastman School of Music.

Randall would still have two years of high school, and it was a problem as to where. We thought of sending him to Frankfurt, but friends suggested we send him to a private school in the States.

In March, Randy and I visited four schools in Massachusetts and Connecticut: Berkshire, Taft, Pomfret, and the Gunnery. They were all interested in having him and offered some scholarship money. Randy decided on Taft School, and that proved to be a very happy choice for him. He played football, sang in the glee club, took classical guitar lessons, and wrote for their magazine.

Mary went with us to Spain and attended Marymount International School in Barcelona for grades 9-11. Melissa went to first through third grades in Bilbao.

In April I was assigned to the Consular Affairs course at the Foreign Service Institute in Washington, DC. I also took Spanish lessons at the Institute to bring the little Spanish I had learned at the University of North Carolina up to a useful level. On May 28 we went up to New York and to Cornwall.

Central Bilbao with US Consulate (A), Bilbao City Hall (B), and former shipyards (C), now the location of the Bilbao Guggenheim Museum.

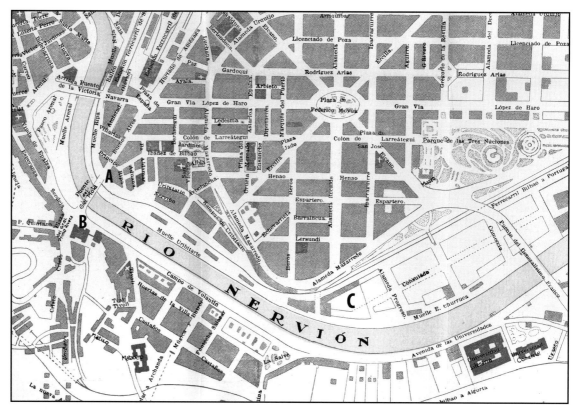

View of Bilbao City Hall across the Nervión River from the US Consulate.

The Consulate was on the second floor of this building at Ibáñez de Bilbao 2.

On May 31, I sailed on the *S.S. Constitution*, thus missing Erica's graduation from high school on June 12. Maria, Mary, and Melissa would follow me to Spain later in the summer.

I arrived in Algeciras, across the bay from Gibraltar, on June 6, and in Madrid on June 7. I was welcomed by my immediate boss, Ralph Blake, the Consul General in Madrid. After a week-end in Madrid I took an overnight train to Bilbao, arriving June 11. I was met by the personnel of the Consulate and was installed at the Hotel Carlton.

In Bilbao I was to replace Bill Rehfeldt, who took me around for a week or so to meet officials and friends. I had two Vice-Consuls on my staff. Joe Livornese did economic reporting, and Peter Simon was in charge of visas and such. Jay Castillo was head of the USIS office across the street from the Consulate, which was located at Ibáñez de Bilbao 2.

From my office window I could see the bridge over the Nervión, a river thick and colored a light chocolate from all the industrial waste in it. Bilbao is a city of much industry, iron, coal, ship-building, chemicals, and rubber. At that time Bilbao was the capital of the Basque country, although Guernica was the older capital [and has since become the Basque capital again].

My Consular district consisted of ten provinces: the three Basque provinces of Vizcaya (Bilbao), Guipúzcoa (San Sebastián), and Alava (Vitoria); and the Spanish provinces of Navarra (Pamplona), Santander, Burgos, Palencia, Logroño, León, and Oviedo.

Before leaving for Bilbao, Mother and I went into New York City to buy shoes. Having rather large feet, we would not be able to find shoes in Spain. It wasn't easy for a still-growing teenager to get shod for the next two years until our next home leave.

At one post, Bilbao or Montevideo, I had to have a pair of shoes custom-made. The first step was to make a wooden mold, or last, and that in just one specific style.

Mary

View from apartment looking toward the river, away from the bay. The apartment was on the third and fourth floors.

After disembarking in Algeciras, near Gibraltar, Mother, Melissa, and I took an overnight train to Madrid, where Dad met us.

Our train was coal-fired and lacked air conditioning; very soon we discovered that we would get vile smoke in our compartments every time we went through a tunnel unless we closed our windows.

It being July, the tunnels were stifling hot! And how to know a tunnel was coming up?

Later, much to my relief, when I took the train from Barcelona to Bilbao on school vacation, that line had a modern train.

Mary

Dad's district included most of northern Spain. In fall 1957 he made a trip through his district. Mother, Melissa, and I came along. There were official welcome meetings and dinners in the main cities as far as Oviedo in Asturias. Galicia wasn't in his district, so Gijón was as far as we went west along the Bay of Biscay. I remember a picnic in a beautiful mountainous region called Picos de Europa (Peaks of Europe) in the Cordillera Cantábrica. Much more fun than official dinners!

Mary

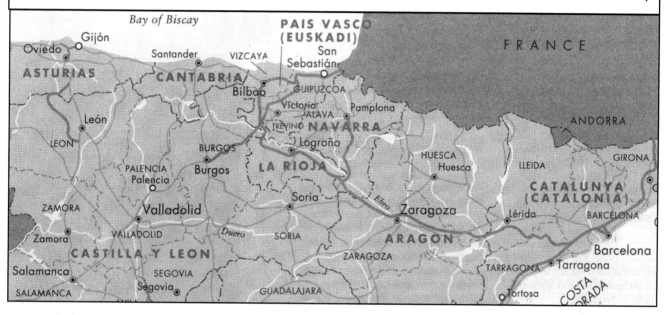

"Euskadi" is the Basque name for the region; "Pais Vasco" is the Spanish name, "Country of the Basques."

The chauffeur drove us all to San Sebastián because Ambassador Lodge's aide had called and said the Amb. would like Daddy and himself to make their official calls together. We got there by 11:00 a.m. after a lovely ride along the coast. We dropped Dad off at the Amb's house and we received an invitation to dinner at 9:00 p.m. I wasn't sure if Missy & I were invited, but we went. Then Mom, Missy & I had a bite at the California Bar Restaurant. We walked the promenade and saw shops and the cathedral. We then met Dad and had lunch at the Hotel. We then went up to the top of the mountain at the bay and saw the view of San Sebastián. We rested at the Hotel in the room of the Amb's secretary and went to dinner. I met Beatrice who went to Marymount and found out about the school. We drove back to Bilbao that night.

Mary's Travel Journal, August 13, 1957

Ralph lighting a cigarette for Maria Teresa Rey, wife of the Cuban Consul.

During my first weeks I visited the Civil and Military Governors of all of these provinces. I also paid courtesy calls on mayors and bishops. In Bilbao itself I made official calls on all the consular representatives of the other countries.

The British Consul was Stanly Burt-Andrews. Jacques Honoré was the French Consul. Ferdinando, Barone de San Severino, was the Italian Consul; and René Rey, who became a close friend, was the Cuban Consul – after Castro took over, René stayed in Bilbao, refusing to return to Cuba. Benjamin Salamanca represented Colombia; and Luis Henrique, Chile. The head of the Bilbao Consular Corps was D. Carlos Pinho Guedes Pinto.

Walkway above the beach in Algorta.

Many of the countries had named Spanish citizens as their Honorary Consuls. Many of them became our very close friends. Foremost among these were Antonio Menchaca (Peru), and Carlos Arechevala (Costa Rica). Consuls arriving later included our cherished friends Carlos Alberto Cava (Argentina), Jorge Cruz Salazar (Guatemala), Rocco Stani (Italy), and Werner Kick (West Germany).

Maria, Mary, and Melissa arrived August 11. We settled down in an apartment in Algorta, at 2 Calle Iglesias. Algorta is a suburb on the coast, overlooking the Bay of Biscay. From our top-floor apartment balcony we always had a wonderful view of the Bay.

Melissa entered the first grade at Sacred Heart School in Algorta. The classes were all in Spanish, which created some difficulty at first, but she was soon speaking Spanish like a native.

One day Dad and we kids had lunch at a terrace restaurant overlooking the beach at Algorta. For dessert, the waiter gave us our choice: flan, cake, or pineapple. We chose pineapple, and each of us was served two slices of canned pineapple.

It all seemed very normal until Dad got the bill. Canned pineapple, apparently being very exotic, cost a fortune! After that, we stuck to flan.

Mary

Rambla was our dog in Bilbao. Her official name was Rambla de las Flores de Cataluña. Such a lengthy, distinguished name for a lively pet who was bought in Barcelona on the Rambla de las Flores. The Rambla is a large pedestrian avenue where vendors of all kinds sell their goods.

Among all the flowers, animals, birds, toys, and other artifacts, Rambla caught my eye and my heart. I pleaded with Mother to buy her, promising to take good care of my new pet. I was 9 years old and for the most part did as well as a 9-year-old could.

Rambla's favorite activity was digging holes in the beach in Algorta, just down the hill from our apartment. We often laughed, watching her "dig a hole to China." I don't think I really understood what that meant, but I always checked the hole to be sure she wasn't going someplace I was not allowed to go.

Melissa

Melissa in her school uniform on the fourth-floor deck of the apartment. The steeple of San Ignacio is in the background.

Priests walking down a street in Barcelona.

Mary Johanna at Marymount International School in Barcelona.

Mary studied at Marymount International School, a finishing school in Barcelona. The emphasis was on teaching the Spanish girls English, so Mary had no difficulty and soon became quite properly Spanish.

In October I took Mary to her school in Barcelona. I had planned to return via Valencia, along the Mediterranean Coast. I was somewhat mystified by the fact that the hotel in Barcelona was unable to get through to reserve me a room in Valencia.

At noon I discovered the reason. As I was having lunch in Benicarló, I met a Spanish couple who had just left Valencia. They said that Valencia was flooded by heavy rains, and they had just been able to escape. I changed my plans and left Benicarló in the direction of Zaragoza.

Before Alcañiz I was overtaken by the heaviest downpour of rain I have ever experienced. The water was cascading off the terraced vineyards. At one point I came to a flooded *arroyo*, where the highway passed through without a bridge.

I met a car which came through, so I felt sure I could also get across. About half-way across my motor stalled.

I felt panicky for a moment, imagining being swept downstream in my new car. Luckily the motor started again, and I crossed safely and got to Zaragoza for the night. The news the next day said that 18 inches of rain had fallen in the area I had passed through.

The Basque dish *bacalao al pil-pil* is made with salt cod, garlic, peppers and olive oil, served here in a *cazuela*, a typical Spanish casserole.

As a child I didn't see much of my mother. Most of my time was spent with the hired help: cooks, maids, and general help.

In Spain we had a housekeeper, Daniela Ayo, and two young girls as the cook and the maid.

The most interesting concoction I distinctly remember them brewing was fish soup – with the whole fish. That was okay – but the fascination for me was watching them eat the fish eyes! I didn't indulge in that delicacy, and even now the thought of it is not appetizing.

What fascinated the Spanish servants was Randy's habit of putting tomato ketchup on everything – including the eggs at breakfast. This custom was definitely American.

Melissa

We loved Spanish cooking. Our apartment in Algorta had an old-fashioned coal stove and I think a modern one as well. We also had an old-fashioned ice box, set in an exterior wall so the ice block melted to the outside, and a modern refrigerator.

Our Spanish cook made wonderful food for us, such as *tortilla española* (potato omelet), *merluza en salsa verde* (hake in green sauce), and *porusalda* (leek soup).

What we found really strange was the heavy use of olive oil, even for frying bacon!

Mary

Merluza or hake at the market.

242

Left: *Calamares en su tinta* (squid cooked in its own ink).

Right: *Merluza en salsa verde* (hake in green sauce).

The *sardineras*, women who sold freshly caught sardines, were quite a sight. One day a woman whose route covered our street in Algorta, was being observed from the top floor of our apartment by yours truly.

Her enormous basket – which she balanced on her head – was full of fish, brimming over with fresh sardines, a local Basque favorite. Much to my surprise, she lost her balance and the load of fish which she carried on her head came crashing to the ground.

No injuries were incurred but a burst of laughter from the top balcony was enough to embarrass the fisher woman.

The *sardinera* has long since disappeared, as the former abundance of sardines has diminished. A statue to the *Sardinera* has been erected near the *transbordador* (see page 270) as a memorial to a well-balanced entrepreneur.

Melissa

In the countryside near Bilbao: above, panorama and wheat-threshing; below, a farmhouse.

I spent the summer after my college freshman year in Bilbao. Dad decided to teach me how to drive a car. For my first lesson he took me out on a quiet road that had only a few burros, bicycles, and carts on it.

Dad said to me, "The first thing you must learn to do is stop the car. So step on the gas, then put on the brakes." I practiced this over and over, and we careened down the road, barely missing the burros and carts. It was scary!

Erica

Learning to drive – on the street and on the golf course

Dad arranged golf lessons for his three oldest children. It was awkward for me at first because we could not find left-handed golf clubs in Spain.

I learned why when I took a train trip to Madrid with him. I started writing in my travel journal on the train. To my surprise the passengers sitting near me all got up and moved to the other end of the car. Dad said that when the Spaniards saw me writing with my left hand they thought I was a witch!

Erica

Jai alai is similar to handball, but the ball must be caught and thrown in one fluid motion. The ball moves so fast that *jai alai* is known as "the game of dodging death" or "ballet with bullets."

The Consulate in Bilbao was always a busy place. It issued a lot of visas to travellers from that area to the United States, mostly to businessmen, but there were two groups which were special.

Ranchers in western States sent representatives to Bilbao and the Basque Country to hire sheep herders, who were then brought to the Consulate for visas. For several weeks at a time, the hallways of the Consulate would reek of the smell of sheep. The sheep herders were then sent to California, Arizona, Wyoming, or Idaho.

They were to work for three or four years and then to return to Spain. Many, however, did not return, or managed somehow to get back to the States. I am told that over half the inhabitants of Boise, Idaho, are of Spanish Basque origin.

The other special group who came for visas were the *jai alai* players. It was not unusual for one of them to drive up in front of the Consulate in a big American car, and with a blonde American wife, to get a visa to work in Florida as a *jai alai* player.

Many Spanish inhabitants of northern Spain had lived for years in the States and then returned home to retire. Every month the Consulate received Social Security checks for Spaniards throughout the Consular district.

The Consulate also performed certain functions for US citizens who travelled to that part of Spain. There were several instances of accidental deaths of Americans travelling in the district.

Running of the bulls through the streets. People follow a bull into the arena and torment him (above), then scatter as the bull gives chase.

On July 7, while Randy and Erica were visiting, we attended the beginning of the week-long festivities for *San Fermín* in Pamplona. Very early in the morning, people were eating garlic soup to sober up after a night of carousing.

Next came the *encierro*, the running of the bulls through the streets to get them from their pens to the bullring.

In the afternoon there were bullfights and then more carousing before starting over the next day.

Mary

The Consulate then had to have the bodies embalmed and shipped to the US. There was one particular incident which I shall never forget.

I was attending the bullfights in Pamplona with some Spanish friends when I was told of an American youth who had been arrested for running over an old woman who was delivering milk along the highway.

The boy and a friend had driven down through France to Pamplona. They had no reservation for lodging, so they did as so many Pamplona visitors do – they stayed up all night, joining the crowds of merry-makers who partied all night. The two boys got separated. In the early morning, one of them took the car to drive out into the country and take a nap somewhere. He fell asleep at the wheel and ran over and killed the woman with the milk cart.

When the Ambassador, Henry Cabot Lodge, heard of the incident, he found that the boy was the son of a friend of his in Washington. When the Ambassador learned that I was in Pamplona, he told me to visit the boy in jail and to visit the Judge to see what could be done. It rather spoiled my day.

It was only after several days of messages from a Spanish lawyer and from the boy's father that it was arranged to release the boy on bail of a couple of thousand dollars – which were to be paid to the old woman's husband. The American boy was then allowed to leave Spain. At the time, it was assumed that if he ever returned to Spain, he could still be tried for the offense.

Randy and Mary in Pamplona.

Clockwise from top left:
Mosque in Sevilla; Roman aqueduct in
Segovia; Ralph at Roman ruins in Valladolid;
Street scene in Sevilla; archways in Mérida;
and monkey on car in Gibraltar.

The Consulate did economic reporting through one of the Vice-consuls and a Spanish local employee, Ramón Solla. All of these activities came under my jurisdiction and direction, so I was engaged in them myself to a certain extent. My more special duties were representation and political reporting.

Representation was a constant thing, a matter of constant contact with Spanish officials of all the ten provinces of my district. I had to be present on many official Spanish occasions, including many holiday functions. It seems that all these functions included a Mass or Te Deum at the Cathedral, followed by a *vino de honor* – an official reception with food and wine. Many of these occasions involved formal banquets.

Political reporting included, as a special feature, the activities of Basque Separatists, who opposed the Madrid Government. This has been a prominent feature of the three Basque provinces for centuries.

In 1958 Erica and Randall spent the summer with us. We had a good time together, and managed to take a trip of several weeks through most of Spain – Burgos, Madrid, Salamanca, Sevilla, Mérida, Algeciras (Gibraltar), Málaga, Granada, and Toledo. Randall had learned to play the guitar so well that we bought him a proper Spanish one.

Also in the summer of 1958, the American Ballet Theater performed at the Santander Festival. Since the Ambassador attended, I had to arrange a big reception to have him and Mrs. Lodge meet all the Spanish dignitaries of that area and the Director of the Ballet.

Mary under a tamarisk tree in San Sebastián.

Above left: Ralph and Maria at a reception. Right: Consular Officers' meeting in Madrid with Ambassador Lodge in center of front row; Ralph is second from left in second row. Below left: Ambassador and Mrs. Lodge greeting embassy guest; Ralph in background. Below right: Maria in receiving line next to Ambassador and Mrs. Lodge.

Our good friend Gabriel Gobeo assisted us at the reception by introducing a lot of the Spanish guests whom I did not know very well. Dr. Gabriel Gobeo was a prominent Bilbao surgeon who had married a member of the Royal Family. He was separated from his wife but was unable to divorce her because Spain had no divorce law.

Gabriel had a beautiful seaside villa in Laredo, which we visited frequently. He had a housekeeper and a butler who took care of everything at the villa. (Later on, after we had left Spain, President Lyndon Johnson's daughter Linda stayed at Gabriel's house in Laredo on her trip to Spain.)

About three times a year the Consular officers had a meeting in Madrid. We were always addressed by the Ambassador and the Deputy Chief of Mission. The remainder of the time was under the Consul General at the Embassy, Ralph Blake, who was our immediate boss in Madrid. It was a good time to get acquainted with our counterparts at other Consulates. Brad Braggiotti, the Ambassador's son-in-law, was Consul General in Sevilla.

My favorite Consular officer was Sam Young in Vigo. We were of the same age, but he had had many more Spanish-speaking posts. (He is now retired and living in Mexico.)

Somehow I was the one who knew more of the entertaining night spots of Madrid, so I suggested where we should eat and where to go for entertainment. (I think I first learned about all that from some of my Latin American colleagues in Bilbao.)

Table etiquette in Spain required that we learn how to eat fruit, a typical dessert, with knife and fork. That included apples, oranges, and bananas.

The only thing we were allowed to touch with our hands was grapes, after washing them in the little glass bowl each diner had for that purpose.

Mother and Dad loved to entertain and had all the accoutrements for fine dining, including little red napkins to tuck into ladies' white linen napkins so as not to stain them with lipstick.

How to know where the ladies would sit? By strict protocol!

The lady most honored sat at Dad's right, and the next most honored at his left; the most honored man was at Mother's right, and the next most honored at her left.

Mary

As Consul in Bilbao, Dad had to represent the US at many official functions to which the diplomatic corps was invited. He needed a tux for evening and a morning coat (tails) in grey for daytime occasions.

Mary

Left: Randy at Altos Hornos steel mill.
Below: a steel mill on the Nervión River.

An American destroyer on an official visit to Bilbao.

When several US destroyers visited Bilbao, I took Melissa down the hill to the beach, where she accidentally cut her foot.

I didn't know how I would get her back up the steep hill, so I asked one of the sailors walking the beach in his white US Navy uniform to carry Melissa up for me.

He agreed and felt very proud to help me out, although he was a bit embarrassed when he learned that our father was the American Consul.

Erica

I went once with several of my Bilbao colleagues to spend the whole week at the *Feria de Sevilla*, an annual festival. We took in all the parades and shows, and especially the bull-fights. It was a colorful and entertaining week.

While I was Consul in Bilbao there were several naval visits – French, British, and American. These involved a lot of formal parties with the officers, while the sailors spent their free time exploring the town and visiting the beaches.

We got to be very good friends with the British naval visitors, and they put on a special signalling show for us as they went out into the Bay of Biscay. We stood on our balcony and waved.

Later, when we had a squadron of American destroyers, they heard about the British display, and they gave us an even better show of maneuvers and colors as they went out to sea. The Spanish Comandante de Marina certainly wondered what was going on. It was all good fun.

As American Consul and wife, we were of course part of the social life of Bilbao. We belonged to the Club Náutico, located in the middle of the City, also to the Golf Club, located near us in Neguri. In any case, we were invited to all the official Spanish functions.

At the very beginning I learned a surprising thing about Spanish social language. I had learned that you should always use the formal *Usted* in speaking to important people. So I was using it with all the upper society people we met.

Procession at the bull ring in Bilbao.

The Feminine U.N. is in Bilbao

Thirty-two countries represented in monthly women's meetings

Maria Collins, wife of the US consul in Bilbao, is an intelligent woman of valiant and daring appearance, full of an exuberant personality, which reaches out and teaches without effort. She speaks Spanish that is short, dry, and repetitious, without being concerned that she discusses masculine topics with a feminine touch. She is the true founder, the mother of the idea that the wives and daughters of the consuls of Bilbao should get together at regular meetings with the warmth and taste of family.

The Husbands Have Nothing to do with it....

Gran Via, 18 June 1959

I did participate in some organized activities with Mother, such as taking a nativity set to the children's hospital in Gorliz, Spain. The smell of the hospital was memorable – very clean – but the look of the many infirm children was very sad.

Mother made a speech and presented the nativity set and a bag of candy as gifts. This visit was written up in the local Bilbao paper.

Melissa

While in Bilbao, one of our favorite places to visit as a family was Dr. Gabriel Gobeo's villa in Laredo. Rambla, our German shepherd, always accompanied us. This picture of the reflecting pool in the formal gardens reminds me of the many hours spent there dreaming of wonderful experiences, with Rambla at my side.

In 2005 I returned to Bilbao – the first time since 1960. As we were driving along the coast – Erica, her husband Bill and their granddaughter Michelle – the sign to Laredo jumped out at me. We took a side trip and found Dr. Gobeo's house.

It felt like returning to those magical times of my childhood. When I knocked on the door and the familiar face of Doña Luisa, Dr. Gobeo's former housekeeper, greeted us, it did seem like going back to my home.

Doña Luisa thought I was my mother and asked where the little girl was. When I identified myself as the "little girl" – just 45 years older – the welcome home was undeniable. The reflecting pool with the statue of the Little Mermaid is gone but the beauty of the former villa still remains.

Melissa

Dr. Gobeo's garden ran down to the beach in Laredo
Below: Melissa, Doña Luisa, and her sister in 2005.

Then a good friend, Lina Lorenzo, American wife of Luis Lorenzo, took me aside one day and said that using *Usted* was wrong: it indicated to the person addressed that you considered him to be on a higher social level than yourself and that you were keeping a distance from him. You had to use *tú*, which meant that you and the person addressed were social equals. I have explained this to professors of Spanish. They find it hard to believe, but it was certainly true of Bilbao society.

Maria was quite active in her association with Consular wives at Bilbao. She got them organized for social work and benevolence, and they had regular meetings. The Consular Corps also met regularly, and whenever a Consular official departed, there was always a *despedida*, special dinner or luncheon in honor of the person leaving. On my wall I have a gold-engraved parchment, dated 6 of June 1960, with the signatures of all the Consular officials attending my *despedida*.

Ralph presents Maria to Bilbao Mayor Zuazagoitia while Melissa looks on.

It would take too much space to pay tribute to all our friends in Bilbao. We were entertained many times by Federico Lipperheide and his wife, Milly. He headed a large chemical firm. Gabriel Gobeo entertained us many times at his villa in Laredo, as well as in Bilbao.

We shall never forget a picnic in the mountains when Gabriel had his butler bring all the food along and serve it in style at an old mill. On another occasion he took us and the British Consul and wife on a salmon-fishing trip – not much luck!

Ralph (left) enjoying a two-hour lunch with friends. Everything in Spain shuts down for two hours for lunch and siesta during the heat of midday.

One of many streets named for Hemingway, who set his most famous novels in Spain.

My good friend Martin Aresti had us at his home several times. Toward the end of our stay, he invited me to a bull-fight in Burgos. He was about to take me to a restaurant I knew to be for foreigners and not very good. He did not know about Ojeda, our favorite restaurant right near the Cathedral. It is an unpretentious place but has, or had, all the typical Spanish foods in their proper season. I persuaded him to go there. We had a wonderful meal.

As we were eating, a group of four or five people entered and sat at another table near us. It was Ernest Hemingway with some of his Spanish friends. My friend Martin was duly impressed, and I joked about his not knowing the best place to eat in Burgos.

In May 1959 we were visited by two Foreign Service Inspectors, Crain and Mitchell. It was my first experience of being inspected, but everything went well, especially after Mitchell took me aside the first morning to tell me that Crain was a stickler for clean desks – all desks cleared at lunch and evening, and typewriters covered.

We soon discovered that Crain and Mitchell were quite friendly, and we had a good time taking them around, entertaining them and showing them the sights. As to the sights--we almost always took visitors to see the Altamira caves, near Santander. Certainly anyone interested in cave paintings 20,000 years old would not want to miss them.

Among our visitors in Bilbao was Ray Thurston, who had been with us in Moscow. An especial pleasure was to have Verton and Lyn Queener, from Maryville, as visitors for about a week. We had a great

Ralph with *Zarzuela* operetta singer.

Travel Journal, 1958

Sept. 13

**Bilbao,
Bayonne,
Pau,
Tarbes,
Toulouse**

Left Algorta with Queeners [Verton and Lyn], Mom, and Missy on way to Paris. On up to border and lunch at Bayonne. Drive through Gascony on the edge of the Pyrenees Mts. Bypassed Lourdes. On to Toulouse for the night in Hotel Cia Midi by the station.

I like the gray-roofed French towns and the green landscape covered with leafy trees, the kind people, and their sweet language. It sure is different from Spain but I like each country for what it is. Amazing how the people, land, language, music, etc., of a country belong to itself alone and fit it perfectly. I like each one for what it is.

Sept. 20-21

**Paris,
Angoulême,
Bilbao**

Mom came by the Sciaky's house at 9:00 a.m. to pick me up. Sorry to leave after having such a nice time with such congenial people. We traveled south through Chartres, Tours, Poitiers, and found a Hôtel Palais in Angoulême to spend the night in.

I sure did have a lot of fun in Paris meeting new people, seeing new places. Each thing new and interesting, so much to learn from each. Take Simone's Uncle John for instance – an FBI man – fought during the war – patience & knows how to handle kids. So much to learn. . . .

Left Angoulême early & traveled south to Bordeaux, where in the Sunday market Mom bought me a pair of wooden *sabots* (shoes) like they wear in the fields. We crossed the border at about lunch time and had lunch at Casa Nicolasa in San Sebastián. Then on to Bilbao.

Oh, it's all finished now. What a wonderful little packet of memories entitled *Paris*. How I wish I could have stayed longer. And I know it could never be the same, nothing ever is the second time. Now to remember it just as it was; the atmosphere and then pack it away again to remember another time this beautiful memory.

Mary, age 14

visit in Spain and then drove them back to Paris for their return voyage. Unfortunately, it was the last time we saw Verton. He died suddenly in New York, on returning to the States.

In July 1959, we returned to the States for three months home leave. Maria, Mary, and Melissa left before me, and I sailed from Algeciras July 5. After a few weeks in Cornwall-on-Hudson, we went to Tennessee. In August we went up to Uncle Max's cottage on Raquette Lake, in the Adirondacks.

Toward the end of August we went down to North Carolina. In September I went with Erica up to the University of Rochester. On the 20th we took Randy up to Harvard.

On August 26 we sailed back to Spain on the *S.S. Independence*. It was partially a cruise, so we went by way of the Azores, landed in Casablanca, took a trip to Rabat by bus, returned to Casablanca, stopped in Algeciras, and spent a day exploring Mallorca.

We disembarked in Barcelona October 5, and were back in Bilbao the next day. On October 15, I took Mary back to Marymount International School in Barcelona for her third year.

In the meantime, there had been changes in our personnel in Bilbao. John Oleson had replaced Peter Simon, and Abraham Hapman had replaced Jay Castillo at America House. Shortly thereafter, Dan Daniels replaced Joe Livornese.

In 1959 Generalíssimo Franco visited Vizcaya for the first time since the Spanish Civil War. There were many festivities to mark the occasion. One of

Ralph with Lyn and Verton Queener and Mary on the northern coast of France.

Bilbao was near France's Basque provinces. We loved to go there, often on day trips, because in France we felt more free and normal. Spain under Franco had many restrictions, such as not speaking the native languages in the provinces, for example Basque in Bilbao or Catalán in Barcelona. Women had to wear modest skirted swimsuits. Imported movies were censored and so cut up that sometimes it was hard to follow the story line.

Mary

Generalíssimo Franco welcoming President Eisenhower to Spain in December 1959. Below: Randy and Mary on the Nervión River.

the highlights of the visit was a procession of boats in the outer harbor.

The Generalíssimo was in an advance boat, and I and some of the lesser officials followed along in another boat, and behind us came all sorts of boats. It was a colorful occasion, followed by an evening dinner at the Club Náutico in Las Arenas.

We decided to spend Christmas of 1959 in Portugal. Because President Eisenhower was going to be in Madrid December 21, we stopped first in Madrid. Leaving Madrid December 23, we spent a night in Trujillo and arrived in Lisbon the following evening.

After a little Christmas celebration in the morning, we went in the afternoon to Estoril and Sintra. The following day we visited the Cosinha Velha in Queluz, where President Eisenhower had visited before Madrid.

The weather in Portugal was so foggy that we decided to go to Sevilla in Spain, where we spent a couple of days. We had dinner with a friend, Gabriel Gonzalez. We then went to Algeciras and Gibraltar, and from there to Almuñecar and Granada, and back to Bilbao on New Year's Eve.

Some other friends of Bilbao were an English couple named Taylor and Mr. Albertson. The Stanis were now there from Italy, and we liked them very much. Another person who was important to us in Bilbao was Elias Segovia, who ran a restaurant-bar and who managed most Consular cocktail parties, as well as catering for official Spanish functions.

Franco's yacht when he visited Bilbao.

When we lived in Bilbao, it was a thriving industrial city with a big steel mill and shipyards, which we visited during the summer of 1958 when Erica and Randy came to visit.

The shipyards were making ocean liners for the Ybarra line. When we left Barcelona for South America in June 1960, we sailed on the Ybarra's *Cabo San Vicente*, which we had visited while it was being constructed in Bilbao.

Mary

The *Cabo San Vicente* in 1960. In 2005 Melissa was visiting the Guggenheim Museum in Bilbao and asked an administrator where the shipyards had been. "Right here," he said.

Shipyard owner doffs his hat as Ralph leaves the shipyards. Ralph's chauffeur, Florenzio, is at right.

In the late 1950s Spain's Ybarra Line commissioned its largest passenger ships yet, the sister ships the *Cabo San Roque* and the *Cabo San Vicente*.

Built in Bilbao, they had a service speed of 20 knots and a capacity of 841 passengers.

Their sailing pattern took them from Genoa and Barcelona to Montevideo and Buenos Aires via Tenerife and Rio de Janeiro.

Vizcaya Bridge

Locally known as the *transbordador*

Vizcaya Bridge (*Puente de Viscaya*, or Bridge of Biscay) is an historic landmark and a World Heritage Site. Located at the mouth of the Nervión River, Vizcaya Bridge links the Bilbao suburbs of Portugalete and Las Arenas.

This bridge is known locally as the *transbordador*, or swing bridge. Ocean-going cargo ships and passenger ships sail underneath while pedestrians and vehicles are ferried across in a gondola which runs continuously 24 hours a day, 365 days a year.

The world's oldest bridge of this type, Vizcaya Bridge was built in 1893 by Alberto Palacio, a disciple of Gustave Eiffel.

Palacio provided an elegant solution to the problem of linking the two sides of the river without disrupting river traffic and without building a massive structure with long ramps.

As can be seen in the picture at the left, the horizontal section of the bridge is not designed to carry traffic but serves instead as a track for the mechanism that conveys the gondola.

Transbordador – literally "ferry" in Spanish – also refers to the gondola, seen in the picture above.

Cars are conveyed in the central open section, and pedestrians ride in the enclosed side sections.

The gondola hangs from cables, and in a strong wind, the *transbordador* really swings!

Ralph, Maria and Melissa waiting in June 1960 for the *transbordador* to return from the opposite bank of the river.

At an Embassy party in Rome, I was amazed to find my Dad conversing in Italian. He had been in Italy right after World War II and still remembered a lot of Italian.

Though I eventually studied many languages myself, I never was able to converse easily in so many as my Dad.

Mary

Mary in Italy during Easter vacation in 1960.

My interest in art began in the spring of 1960, on my trip to Italy with Dad. He knew what was important to see in Tuscany and Rome, and after that, I was eager not only to learn more about the history of art and architecture, but also to learn Italian.

Later that year, after arriving in South America, I started to learn Italian, studying at private institutes in Montevideo, Buenos Aires, and Bogotá in 1961-62.

On our summer trip in 1964, because I was taking some art history courses in college, Dad made sure we saw some of the important art museums in cities along our itinerary, such as St. Louis and Chicago.

Mary

In early February the Department informed me that I was to be transferred to Montevideo, Uruguay. Although this would not take place until June, the remainder of my stay in Bilbao took on a good-bye aspect. The Livorneses left in March.

In April I took an Easter vacation with our daughter Mary, on a trip to Italy. Martin Aresti and his daughter went with me to Barcelona to pick up Mary. They left us at Genoa and went on to Milan. Mary and I spent a night in Siena and arrived in Rome on April 12. We did a lot of sightseeing, all new for Mary: St. Peter's, Pantheon, Colosseo, St. John Lateran, Vatican, Catacombs, Galleria Nazionale, Tivoli, Castel Gandolfo, Frascat, Museo Nazionale, Ostia, and more.

Despedida, farewell dinner for Ralph, center, and Maria, left.

We saw the Listers, who had been in Moscow and were now at the Embassy in Rome. After watching and hearing the Pope give his message from the balcony at St. Peter's, we left Rome, stopping in Assisi and Perugia, then on to Florence for two days, Bologna, Piacenza, and Milan on the 21st.

We visited the Cathedral, the Last Supper and the Fair. We spent a night in Finale Ligure, which had stuck in my mind since my days in Munich in 1932-33, because all the travel advertisements for Italy seemed to mention Finale Ligure. Sure enough, most of the hotels had German guests.

Back in France, we stayed in Nîmes. In Carcassonne we inquired about the snow on the pass through Andorra. Finding the road open – with high masses of snow on both sides, we went through Andorra and spent the night in Spain, in Seo de

Ship officers with Ralph, Melissa, and Maria aboard the *Cabo San Vincente.*

Urgel. The following day, April 24, we were back in Barcelona. The next day I was in Bilbao.

In early May, Maria went to Germany to visit her relatives in the Pfalz. While she was away, I went to Oviedo and Gijón, both in my district, and I was constantly invited out. The Archdeacon Johnston visited the English Church. In early June we had our annual Consulate outing, on the beach of Laredo. The last few days were hectic, with a final party at the Arizona Club, with just about everybody there.

We drove to Barcelona, attended the graduation ceremony at Marymount, and sailed June 14 on the *Cabo San Vicente*. This ship had been built in Bilbao while we were there, and we had attended a cocktail party on board to celebrate its launching. We knew the Captain and felt quite at home on board. On June 16 we left Cadiz, stopped June 18 at the island of Tenerife in the Canary Islands, and June 22 crossed the Equator near St. Paul's Rocks.

Stopping in Rio de Janeiro on June 26, we found, almost next to us, the *S.S. Argentina* from New York, with Erica and Randall aboard! They had left New York June 16. We had a happy reunion and went together to the top of Corcovado, with the Cristo statue, to take in the marvelous view of the Rio harbor. We left Erica and Randall to follow on the *S.S. Argentina*, and arrived the next day in Santos. There we were met by Scott and Nancy Lyon, who had come down from São Paolo to greet us. We arrived in Montevideo the evening of June 29. Erica and Randall arrived July 1.

Melissa, center, playing deck games.

Below left: Maria and Melissa visiting the ship's galley.

Below right: Maria, Melissa, Mary, and Captain Pujana.

"The Captain of the vessel, Don José Pujana, has the honor of inviting you for a welcoming cocktail at 8 PM today in the Salon-Bar. Proper dress is recommended.

En route, 18 June 1960"

YBARRA Y CIA., S. A
«M\n CABO SAN VICENTE»
SEVILLA
—

El Capitán del buque, D. José Pujana, tiene el honor de invitar a Vd. al Cocktail de Bienvenida que tendrá lugar a las 20 horas del día de hoy en el Salón-Bar Se recomienda etiqueta.

En la Mar, 18 JUN 1960

At costume party, Melissa (seated) is Japanese girl, Mary (right) is champagne bottle, behind Maria, who is the mailbag! Below: Ralph doing the limbo with the Captain's wife.

Melissa in center of girls in grass skirts with Queen of the Sea and King Neptune behind her.

Melissa covers her Dad with whipped cream while the Queen of the Sea and King Neptune watch.

King Neptune and Queen of the Sea Maria ruled over the festivities for the Crossing of the Equator.

Left: Maria and Ralph doing the "Apple Dance" with the Captain and his wife.

Right: Claudia Moos and Erica Collins, cabin mates on the *S.S. Argentina*, went to their costume party dressed as "Night and Day" in costumes of their own creation, and won third prize.

I was up early the day the *S.S. Argentina* sailed up the river to Rio de Janiero, en route to Montevideo. Watching from the deck, I spotted the *Cabo San Vicente* ahead of us.

That was the ship my family was on! I ran to the bridge and asked if they would radio the *Cabo* and tell my parents we were coming in behind them. They did, and when we docked, there was Dad on the dock waving to us.

He was too far away to hear me, so we communicated by sign language. We had a great reunion in Rio!

Erica

Family reunion on top of Corcovado in Rio de Janeiro. From left: Mary, Erica, Melissa, Randall, Maria.

Montevideo suburbs, showing Avenida Brasil and Boulevard Espãna, where Collins apartments stood.

Uruguay
1960-1963

In Plaza Independencia, Montevideo's main square, people lay wreaths during ceremonies in memory of José Artigas, the father of Uruguayan independence.

Assignment: Montevideo

When we first arrived in Uruguay, we had to stay at the Victoria Plaza Hotel until we could find a place to live. We stayed there for almost three months, occupying three rooms. We had our meals at various restaurants when we were not invited out.

My job at the Embassy was that of First Secretary and Head of the Political Section. We reported on political events and personalities, activities of political parties, labor reactions, and relations with other countries, as well as with the United States.

Because I had had experience with Eastern Europe, I found it interesting to write a history of the Uruguayan Communist Party and a report on the Party's current position in Uruguay. Both of those reports were highly commended by the Department, and no doubt they contributed to my promotion to FSO-2 in April 1963.

I barely missed having Howard Hunt [later of Watergate fame] in my office. He was head of the CIA element in the Embassy, which was nominally part of the Political Section but was behind a separate door beyond the rooms of the Political Section.

When I arrived, the Political Section included Robert C. Hayes, George R. Vitale, and Herbert Mitchell. Hayes reported on labor matters; Vitale, as a long-time resident of Montevideo, was familiar with political and other Uruguayan personalities. Herb,

Mary, Erica, and Randall on street corner at far right, waiting to cross in heavy traffic in downtown Montevideo.

Montevideo had only one or two traffic lights. The car that arrived first at an intersection had right of way.

This was most dramatic at night. Drivers drove without their headlights on! As they approached an intersection, they flashed their lights and drove on through. Our Embassy chauffeur always drove fast and it was very scary, even from the back seat!

Erica

284

who arrived at the same time we did – he was on the same ship as Erica and Randall, specialized in political reporting. We all worked well together.

Once a week, representatives of the Military Attaché's office, the Consular Section, USIA, and so on met in my Office to put together a brief weekly report to the State Department in Washington, called the "Weeka".

The Ambassador was Robert F. Woodward, whom I had met briefly in Stockholm while I was stationed in Moscow. He and his wife, Virginia, were extremely nice to us, and I enjoyed working for him. The Deputy Chief of Mission was Henry Hoyt, who later returned as Ambassador. The Military Attaché was Col. Earl Macherey. Henry Buckhardt (wife Mary Elizabeth) was the Agricultural Attaché.

Harold Urist, a classmate of mine at the University of North Carolina in 1930, was Head of the USIS office. Joseph Sagona was Administrative Officer. George Landau was Head of the Economic Section and was later Ambassador to Paraguay, Chile, and Venezuela. Among the other members of the Embassy staff were Thomas Flores, Edward Purcell, Daniel Garcia, Samuel Hart, and Richard Tucker.

Mary had still a year of high school to finish. The high school in Uruguay did not have a laboratory for science courses so we sent Mary to the American Community School in Buenos Aires. She stayed with the Bazians, an American family of Armenian and Lebanese extraction, thereby acquiring her taste for Near Eastern foods.

Plaza Independencia with city in the background.

Dear Friends,

This year we greet you from south of the Equator, from the Republica Oriental de Uruguay, where Ralph is First Secretary and Political Officer at the Embassy. The transfer orders, which brought us here from Bilbao, came as quite a surprise but I must say, a rather pleasant one, since we had long hoped some day to have a South American post. The sadness of leaving Spain and our dear friends was tempered somewhat by the thoroughly enjoyable voyage in one of Spain's most luxurious air-conditioned trans-atlantic liners, the Cabo San Vicente.

We had a warm spot in our hearts for this ship, since we had watched its construction in the shipyard in Bilbao, and a still warmer feeling as we became like "one of the family" among its predominantly Basque officers and crew. Mary and Melissa were with us and took an active part in shipboard life and especially enjoyed the festivities of crossing the Equator at which, I, Maria, reigned as Queen. This "exalted" position did not prevent me from getting tossed into the pool along with all the other neophytes. . . .We stopped in the Canary Islands for a day, which gave us time enough to visit the interior of Tenerife and the enormous banana plantations.

Our greatest delight, however, was upon arriving in Rio de Janeiro, to meet up with Erica and Randy who were traveling on an American ship to join us here. Our family was once again united and, even though after arriving here we spent the length of the children's vacation in a hotel, it was grand being together.

After three months of looking, we finally located an apartment in Pocitos, the closest suburb to Montevideo. Actually, the city strings out along the river so there is a continuous line of buildings along the riverside parkway for about fifteen miles from the center of the city.

Our apartment is situated one block from the beach on one of the principal avenues and has a lovely view in all directions. It is not as large as we would like, but it serves our needs and, most important, is within our rental allowance. Rents have doubled in recent months and adequate housing is becoming very difficult to find. There is a great deal of construction of apartments going on, but they are usually for sale and the rooms so small that they are not suitable for a family with children.

A school for Melissa was not difficult to find, but Mary, as a senior in high school, presented quite a problem until we located the American Community School, called Escuelas Lincoln, in Buenos Aires. This is the only school of its type south of the Equator and is unique in that it offers a curriculum accredited and approved by the Southern Association of High Schools and Colleges and its school year coincides with that of the Northern Hemisphere so children finishing here in July can transfer without loss of credits or time to Stateside schools. The Christmas holiday is also the summer holiday, so soon we will have both Mary and Melissa at home. Then will come the enjoyment of the beaches, of which this coast has many beautiful ones and we hope to travel to the interior of this country and adjoining ones.

Recently, I, Maria, was able to take a trip to the western part of Uruguay as far as Brazil. The roads are for the most part of dirt but well graded. With the exception of fords over some of the streams, I would say that the roads are quite passable. However, when it rains, there is sometimes a slick topping of mud which makes driving hazardous and it is wise to carry along chains for such emergencies. But the great open spaces – with the cattle, horses, sheep, and ostriches peacefully grazing and gauchos herding the cattle – are a beautiful sight to behold.

Especially in the spring, which it is as I now write, the fields are innumerable shades of green and abound with beautiful birds and wild flowers, some of them of a tropical nature, and the truly purple thistle which gives one to understand why Uruguay is so often referred to as the Purple Land. The vast fields of flax with its pale blue flowers moving gently in the breeze create a mirage of quiet waters, the clouds float gently overhead, and there is a great feeling of peace.

1960 has been kind to us. We have made many new friends and renewed old friendships. We reiterate as in the past, since it has been our pleasure that some of you have been able to do so, to come to see us. You will find Montevideo a lovely city and you will make us very happy if you can come for a visit.

To all of you a very Merry Christmas and may the New Year bring you much happiness. Sincerest best wishes,

Maria, Ralph, Mary, and Melissa Collins

The Río de la Plata is about 100 miles wide at its estuary, where Buenos Aires and Montevideo are located.

To travel between the cities, we had to take the ferry between Colonia, on the Uruguayan side, and Buenos Aires; it took several hours. The fastest way across was by float plane from the port of Montevideo to the port of Buenos Aires.

Buenos Aires was like going to Paris, a big fashionable city with a varied cultural life. But Montevideo did have orchestra concerts and plays at the Teatro Solis in the old city.

Montevideo featured a beautiful waterside parkway from downtown out to the suburbs. Each cove had a beach of sorts, and the beaches got better the further down the estuary you went.

Punta del Este, at the opening to the estuary, had the best beaches of all and was a resort town.

Mary

Ferry that Mary took to attend school in Buenos Aires.

288

On August 19, 1960, Erica sailed on the *S.S. Brazil* to return to the States and her final year at the University of Rochester. Randy wanted to fly back to the States, returning for his second year at Harvard, so he left September 2, flying via Santiago, up the west coast of South America.

September 27 we left the Hotel Victoria Plaza and moved into an apartment at Avenida Brasil 3074, 8th floor, in the Pocitos area of Montevideo. From our front balcony we looked out over the beach on the Río de la Plata. Most of the Embassy personnel lived in the suburb of Carrasco, also on the beach, and near the airport.

Our first year was a time for getting a good look at a different part of the world. Uruguay was mostly flat, with beaches all the way from Montevideo to the Brazilian border. We had seen Punta del Este from the ship on our arrival, and we went there several times in the first year, usually on Sunday afternoons. We spent a holiday on the beach near the Brazilian border.

We went inland to Minas and Durazno. We became familiar with the large haciendas and the flocks of sheep and the gauchos! Montevideo had an active cultural life, and we also got across to Buenos Aires frequently.

In July 1961, Mary graduated from the American Community School in Buenos Aires. She had been accepted at the University of Pennsylvania, but she decided that she would like to go to the Universidad de los Andes in Bogotá, Colombia. We had met the University president in Montevideo.

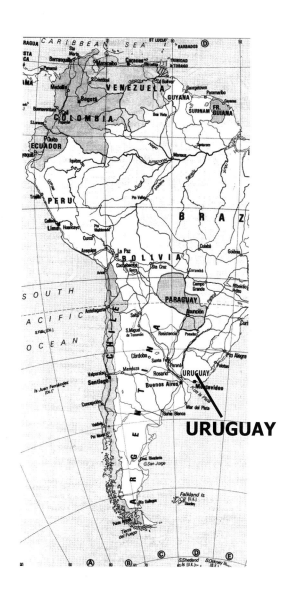

Santa arriving in Montevideo by helicopter on a hot December day.

Melissa, age 11, in December 1961.

Santa's visit was always memorable, filled with the anticipation of receiving some special present from Santa himself who had traveled so far to get to Montevideo. "How did he do it?" I wondered.

My illusion of Santa was tainted when, during one of these visits, I recognized the face behind the false beard and white hair.

As clearly as I could, considering my shock, I boldly said: "You're not Santa. You're Mr. Newell." The imposter insisted on his identity as the traveler from the North Pole but quietly asked me to keep his true identity a secret so as not to influence the younger believers.

Needless to say, I was aghast and promptly told Mother, who explained – as only Mother could do – that Mr. Newell was filling in for Santa as the journey was indeed too long for Santa himself to come during the day. Her response most likely appeased me as I continued greatly appreciating Santa's gifts for many years to come.

Melissa

Because Uruguay is in the southern hemisphere, it was winter time, although we had no extremely low temperatures. As a matter of fact, we had a lot more winters than summers. We arrived in winter, and the following year, after winter in Montevideo, 1961, we had home leave – three months of winter in the States, and after our return to Montevideo we had another winter in mid-1962!

We found Montevideo to be a very friendly place. It seemed that more than half the population of Uruguay lived in the capital – although many people had homes in the countryside.

In October we left Montevideo for three months of home leave, traveling on the Delta Line *S.S. Del Sud*, making stops in Paranaguá, Santos, Rio, and Curaçao. In the first three of these places, the ship took on loads of coffee.

From Santos we went up to São Paulo and spent a night with Scott and Nancy Lyon. In Curaçao we were entertained by the American Consul General, Vic Pallister, whom I had met when he came to the embassy in Moscow as a Foreign Service Inspector.

We spent two nights in New Orleans and traveled from there to Knoxville, making a three-day stop in Maryville to visit with dear old friends – the Alexanders, the Callaways, and many more.

We arrived in Cornwall-on-Hudson, NY, November 9. After a week there, we went on down to Greenville, NC, for another family visit.

At the end of November I went by bus to Indianapolis and Bloomington to visit Erica at

Melissa's party on her 11th birthday.

Individual Americans Can Bring Security In Foreign Relations

By DR. RALPH S. COLLINS

With the memories of World War II and the Korean War still fresh in the minds of all American citizens, it is obvious that international relations play a very important role in the security of every American family and community.

It is no longer seriously suggested by anyone that the people of the United States can be unconcerned with the problems of other peoples in other nations, although it is easier to shut our eyes to such things and to devote our attention to our own domestic problems and to the enjoyment of the comforts of a high standard of living. Aware as we are of the impossibility and even irresponsibility of any such position, every American citizen must seek to understand the complications of our international relations and to make his own contribution toward world peace and friendship.

In the world of the 60s, the most important fact in international relations is the unfortunate division of the world into two opposing camps; the democratic and totalitarian, with certain uncommitted countries in between. On the one side there are the countries which believe in the primacy of spiritual values, the worth of the individual and the forms of democracy which preserve those ideals. On the other, the Communist totalitarian bloc denies the spiritual nature of man and seeks to impose a soulless mechanism of control which serves an all-powerful state and destroys individual freedom. In such a struggle, our place is obvious. Moreover, we must assume the leadership of the democratic bloc and, therefore, must give our very best to assure that this leadership is effective and beneficial to the peoples of the world.

(EDITOR'S NOTE: Dr. Collins' article written for The Times' special edition, Security in the 60s, was delayed while being checked for routine clearance by the State Department and was not received in time for publication with the remainder of the section Tuesday.)

In attempting to perform our duties and obligations in international relations, we are faced with a double problem. On the one hand, we cannot cut ourselves off from dealing with the opposing Communist bloc. Although our experiences in this have been very discouraging and frustrating, we must always keep open the avenues of negotiation and the possibilities of reaching agreemnt on curcial differences.

On the other hand, our relationships with the countries on our own side, supporters of the same democratic ideals, are not always simple. Misunderstandings and distrust arise to make our common efforts more complicated. The goal of preserving world peace and creating a better future for all people makes our best efforts supremely important.

In our relations with the Communist bloc of nations, our primary purpose is to reach peaceful solutions to conflicts which could seriously endanger world peace. In the first place, we must be ready, at all times, to defend ourselves and to assure the survival of our democratic form of life in case the worst comes about. We must, therefore, have military capabilities second to none.

On the other hand, our Government is attempting to reduce tensions and to reach agreements which would reduce the possibility of ultimate conflict and which would, in the end, we hope, lead to the restoration of democratic processes throughout the

Former Professor Serves State Department

Dr. Ralph S. Collins, now first secretary of embassy, Montevideo, Uruguay, was Associate Professor of Modern Languages at Maryville College from 1935 to 1945.

Born Nov. 1, 1910 at Grifton, N. C., he received his A. B. degree from the University of North Carolina in 1930 and his M. A. there in 1931. In 1938 he received his Ph.D. degree from John Hopkins University.

Since he joined the United States Department he has served as Foreign Service Officer in Berlin (1946-48), Moscow (1949-51), Frankfurt (1952-54), Department of State (1954-57), and Bilbao, Spain (1957-60).

DR. RALPH COLLINS

Dr. Collins still maintains his legal residence in Blount County.

world. The most important means for achieving this goal are peaceful in nature and are based upon the increased mutual understnading of peoples. For this reason, the free exchange of information, and a wide exchange-of-persons program, are very important, because we feel that if the artificial barriers between the two world blocs can be broken down, the peoples on both sides will find, because of common interests and through increased understanding, that they want the same kind of a world. This does not necessarily mean that we can convert the peoples now under Communist control to adopting our specific types of government, but we can hope that through evolutionary processes the materialistic totalitarian system of government cannot survive the peoples' desire for freedom and for spiritual and cultural values.

In our relationships with the countries of the free world, we also have many problems preventing mutual understanding and full cooperation for the preservation of freedom and democracy. It is not inherent in our system of government and our way of conducting international relations that we can form a monolithic bloc under the control of one government, such as the Communist world attempts to create.

Although other free countries of the world look to us for leadership, they demand that we treat them as equals. We must, therefore, rely on our common traditions, our common sense of values, and our common interests in resisting the encroachment of totalitarian ideals, in order to achieve community of policy and action. Voluntary cooperation among the freedom-loving peoples of the world is an essential element of our common democratic way of life, and only thorough it can we reach our ideal of a world of peace and well-being for all peoples.

Since the peoples of other free countries of the world do look to us for leadership, the way of life which we have developed in the United States tends to symbolize for these people the strengths and weaknesses of the free and democratic system as opposed to the regimented communist system. Because peoples in other countries hope that we will symbolize as perfect a system as possible, they are deeply disappointed when they perceive anything in the United States which seems to be a flaw in our way of life. Our country is criticized by its greatest admirers, even though the defects which are criticized may seem insignificant to us as compared with similar defects in the countries of the persons who are criticizing us. This gives all United States citizens a special responsibility in trying to make "the image of the United States" as perfect as possible.

It makes it especially important for us all to try to avoid any action or attitude which may appear Undemocratic, and it makes it especially important that we all contribute in every way we to building a system that will truly afford a decent opportunity to every man, woman and child in our great country. Fortunately, great progress has been made in reaching these idealistic goals, but there is still much work to be done within the United States, and the people who accomplish this will be doing more to win the lasting friendship and cooperation of foreign peoples than can be done by any diplomat abroad.

The very size and wealth of the United States is sometimes the cause of distrust* and envy. For instance, among the countries who are our neighbors in Latin America, we find that there is a certain amount of anti-U. S. feeling, which stands in the way of complete understanding and cooperation. Because of our wealth and power, many of our neighbors fear that if they follow our leadership too closely, they may lose their own national identity, that they would be swept along on international ventures which they have misgivings about.

In the desire to preserve their own traditions and values, they sometimes accuse us of being materialistic. Therefore, in our relationships with our neighbors, particularly in Latin America, we must always attempt to understand their point of view and maintain absolute respect for their national feelings. We must avoid all appearances of interference in their international affairs. Most important of all, we must try to meet them on their own level. As individuals, we must meet them without false pride and with a genuine desire to understand and to cooperate.

The number of individual citizens of the United States who find the possibility of making a direct contribution to international understanding through associations with foreign peoples in their own countries or in the United States may not be very large, but the number is increasing constantly. More and more Americans find it possible to travel abroad, and many people come from other countries to visit us. Even those of us who do not find it possible to travel abroad, nevertheless have the opportunity through newspapers, books, radio and television to learn about other peoples and to increase our understanding of world problems. In this way, every citizen can make a contribution to good international relations and to the security of the free world.

The awful consequences of failing to achieve these goals make it the duty of every one of us to be better informed about world problems, to try to understand other peoples of the world and, whether we travel abroad or remain in the United States always to exemplify the democratic ideals we cherish. Thus each one can make an important contribution to the security of his country and of the democratic world in the 60s and in the further decades to come.

Ralph's article in the *Maryville-Alcoa Times*, March 2, 1961.

Clockwise from top left: Beach in front of apartment, looking north; beach, looking south; Maria on the beach in July, winter in the Southern Hemisphere; Randall, Mary, and Erica at seaside at Punte del Este, in August (winter); apartment on Bulevar España; the beach in winter.

Ranchers, left, and gauchos, above, in rural areas. Below: Melissa poses with a gaucho.

The Burkhardts, our good friends in Uruguay, often had us accompany them to *estancias*, or ranches, for livestock auctions. These events always featured an *asado*, or barbeque.

Unlike barbeques in the US, *asados* featured whole lambs split down the middle and roasted on an open fire. Also, the beef in Uruguay and Argentina was the very best we have ever eaten.

The popular drink was *hierba maté*, a South American tea drunk from a small gourd through a *bombilla*, a silver straw with a little rounded sieve at the bottom.

The gourd held the tea leaves, and then hot water from a thermos was poured onto the leaves periodically. How strange for us to see people at the beach drinking *maté*.

Mary

Honor guard outside the Palacio Legislativo.

Indiana University, where she was studying for an MA in Music Theory. Then, a week before Christmas, we went up to Cambridge to bring Randy home from Harvard. We were all together for Christmas – for the first time in five years!

On January 3, 1962, we left New York on a Pan-American flight and were back in Montevideo the next day – one of the fastest trips we had ever made between the States and a foreign post!

1962 was a year for changes at the Embassy in Montevideo. Ambassador Woodward left and was replaced by Edward Sparks. We missed the Woodwards, and eventually we established a good relationship with the Sparkses.

Sparks was serving his last assignment as Ambassador, and when he retired in July, I was for one day Chargé d'Affaires ad interim – until Don Zook, the Deputy Chief of Mission, returned from vacation. Later that month, on July 27, Wymberley Coerr arrived as Ambassador and presented his credentials to the Uruguayan government.

Among other changes in the Embassy family: Lemuel Graves replaced Hal Urist at USIS; Louis Mark and Brewster Hemenway arrived in April, and George and Marie Landau left May 1. Our good friends Bob and Grace Hayes had left in February.

In June I went to Bogotá to spend a week and to accompany Mary from the University of the Andes back to Montevideo. Our Moscow friends Jim and Vaughn Pratt were in Bogotá – Jim was a Foreign Service Inspector at the time.

Parade passing the American Embassy.

297

Visit to Machu Picchu. Above: Mary in a *ruana*, or cape.

Below: Ralph is seated third from right.

Llamas in Peru.

That meant that there were lots of parties for the Inspectors, and I was included. One of the Embassy personnel there was Ethel Balashova, who had worked for our Embassy in Moscow while we were there. Vaughn and I did a lot of sightseeing together. Mary and I stopped in Lima for a few days, and took the trip to Cuzco and Machu Picchu, which we enjoyed very much.

Back in Montevideo, we persuaded Mary to transfer to a university in the States. We felt that the social restrictions on single girls, which prevail all over South America, were too confining for her.

Because it was mid-summer, we did not have the possibility of formal applications, so I wrote to my old Carolina classmate Pete (Cecil P.) Taylor, who was Dean of Liberal Arts at Louisiana State University, and asked if he could take care of Mary if we sent her up.

He arranged everything, and Mary left for Baton Rouge on September 10, 1962. In the meantime Pete had been made Chancellor of the LSU campus in Baton Rouge. On the LSU faculty was my colleague from Marburg and Berlin days, John T. Krumpelmann.

Mary left for Baton Rouge on September 10. She received her Bachelor's degree in French Language and Literature from Louisiana State University in 1965.

In 1962 I was on the Montevideo Fulbright Commission, which had regular meetings. One of the Uruguayan members was a former Foreign Minister. I found the assignment interesting.

Mary and Ralph deplaning in Cuzco, Peru.

Mother and Dad went to receptions, dinners, or parties almost every night of the week, but very few of these were casual or fun get-togethers with friends. Instead they were diplomatic events at which attendance was required.

Beforehand Mother and Dad received a list of who would attend so they could study the list and decide to whom they should talk and what they should talk about. Parties such as these were not for fun – they were for work!

Erica

Maria is greeted by the Canadian Ambassador to Uruguay.

I have been taking Mimi (Mary) with me to various parties, and this week was a rather busy one. We went to a Polish reception Monday, to a cocktail party given by a French diplomat on Tuesday, to a Japanese reception Wednesday, and last night to a Fulbright Commission party for a group of students from the Western College for Women in Oxford, Ohio.

Letter from Ralph to Erica
July 26, 1963

Ezra Taft Benson, right, US Secretary of Agriculture, is welcomed at Carrasco Airport by the Collins family, the Speaker of the Uruguayan House of Representatives, and the Deputy Chief of Mission of the American Embassy.

Above: Plaque at Punta del Este honoring President John F. Kennedy, left, at the Alliance for Progress meeting; Jackie Kennedy stands at center. Below: Kennedy addressing the Alliance for Progress delegates.

One of the events of my last year at Montevideo was the Alliance for Progress meeting at Punta del Este, with Dean Rusk and President Kennedy attending. That kept the whole Embassy busy for a while.

After that, we were all busy reporting on the Uruguayan national elections. Among the candidates was an interesting person, Michelini, who was considered by some to be quite radical; later, he was killed in Buenos Aires, during the military dictatorship there and in Uruguay. Jorge Battle, whom I had gotten to know fairly well, was elected to the ruling Council, and President of the same.

A social highlight was the November wedding of Bunny Graves, who became a good friend of Mary's. We all liked the Graves family very much.

Among the Congressional visitors were Senator Inouye from Hawaii and a Congressman from New York. Secretary of Agriculture Ezra Taft Benson visited in 1960. Governor Ernest Hollings of South Carolina visited Montevideo in 1961.

On October 1, 1962, we moved from the apartment on Avenida Brasil to a new building at #2904 Bulevar España. It was a short distance away, so we were still in Pocitos, with a view of the beach. The new apartment had a very nice room for big parties, and we enjoyed living there.

On January 28, 1962, Randall married Mary Bryson Dean, whom he had met at Harvard. We could not go to Boston, Massachusetts, for the wedding, but Erica and Mary, who were both in college in the States, attended.

Maria and Mary dressed for a reception.

Maria and Ralph hosting a party in their apartment with the Guatemalan Ambassador to Uruguay and his wife. On the wall is a painting they bought in Moscow.

For about a month now I've had a conversation going at parties with the Uruguayan Minister of Defense about a replica of the Statue of Liberty on a building downtown. My question is whether she has a crown or a hat. I know perfectly well it is a crown, but whenever the Minister and I meet, we get started on this, and since he hasn't seen the statue, he asks everybody else around. It makes for the liveliest conversation because it puts everybody local on the defensive and very few like to admit that they don't know.

Letter from Maria to Erica, August 12, 1962

Dear Mary,

Montevideo

May, 1963

Your letter arrived yesterday. It coincided with the Wednesday Pan-Am flight to Montevideo. There are now two flights a week, Sunday and Wednesday, so any letter that makes them arrives here very promptly.

Mother is now planning to leave here May 23. She will spend the night in São Paolo and will fly the next day to Guatemala, via Brasilia and Panama. She will stop in Guatemala and Mexico City, flying from there to New Orleans. She will let you know when she will arrive in New Orleans. I presume it will be by May 30. . . .

I hope you do well on your exams and that you are happy with the results of the year. Mother will travel with you to New York and the two of you will have the pleasure of attending Randy's Harvard graduation. Maybe Granny and Grandaddy can go too. I'm sorry I can't be there, but there just isn't the time and money available to allow me to make the trip.

I appreciate the fact that you wanted very much to come to Montevideo during your vacation, but I am afraid I just can't afford to pay for the travel. Also Mother will probably be in New York until the end of June. Anyway, the following summer you can visit us, wherever that may be, and Montevideo can hardly be too exciting for you anymore.

A few weeks ago I learned the name of my replacement here. . . . he is to arrive here in January. That doesn't seem so far off, so I am full of speculation as to where I shall be assigned next.

Yesterday the Uruguayan peso left its official rate and fell to 13.60 to the dollar. It may continue to fall and eventually we will have a new rate. It is welcome since prices have continued to rise here and things get more expensive. The rent I have been paying has been beyond my allowance, so now it may be under for a while. It is at least temporary relief. Somehow the attempt to accumulate enough money to pay Randy's and your bills keeps the budget rather tight. Since Randy is not getting a scholarship at Stanford, I have promised to pay his tuition, $1400.

Love, Daddy

Once while I was gone to pick up Mary Johanna from school in Bogotá, Ralph and Melissa went to visit a friend who had a black and white cocker spaniel. The spaniel had had pups.

Melissa said, "Oh, can't I have one of the puppies?" And Ralph said, "Yes, all right."

When Mary and I returned to Montevideo, I was greeted at the door by this yapping little pup that ran around me. I said, "What in the world is that?"

Melissa said, "Mommy, I can keep her, I can keep her, can't I? Please, please, please." Well, by that time it was too late to say no because the puppy had become a member of the household.

Maria, our Uruguayan maid, helped take care of the puppy, which we called "Chinela," Little Slipper. She had pedigree papers and her name was Annabelle Glisson de Wales.

In 1963 when we returned to the States, Ralph agreed that we could bring Chinela with us. She became the darling of the household. She understood Spanish and English commands. She was our bilingual dog. . . .She was a faithful and loving dog.

Maria Collins

When we got Chinela she was the liveliest of her litter and could fit in my Dad's hand. She was so small and very cute. Chinela was in many pedigree dog shows with her mother and other sisters in Uruguay. I remember being able to participate in the shows as her owner. It was always a proud moment when all of them would win their red ribbons. Chinela traveled back to America with us and enjoyed being the family pet. I took pride in having her pose for any photographic moment, remembering our showcase days.

Melissa

As I remember this last day of school, I recall the pride of holding the American flag. Being the tallest American student had some advantages. But one disadvantage was the very hot day and the fainting spell which the proud flag bearer experienced. That's right – there I was standing at attention during the opening ceremony when I started to teeter. I remember passing the flag to the girl next to me as I staggered to the front office where I promptly fainted.

I was quickly revived by the school secretary, who made me drink a cup of very strong black coffee with lots of sugar. It was my first coffee experience. But the coffee did the trick and I was able to return to my post, seemingly unscathed but mentally more alert.

Melissa

Maria Pricheluzky was our housekeeper in Montevideo. She spent all her time with me and I with her. We went to see *West Side Story* in 1963. She insisted I wear white socks when I left the apartment, which was the standard Mother had set for me. But I quickly changed out of my socks and put on stockings while riding down the elevator, just in time to make my appearance as a young woman as I stepped out of the apartment building into the street. *West Side Story* remains one of my favorite movies and probably has a lot to do with my enjoyment of musical theatre.

Melissa

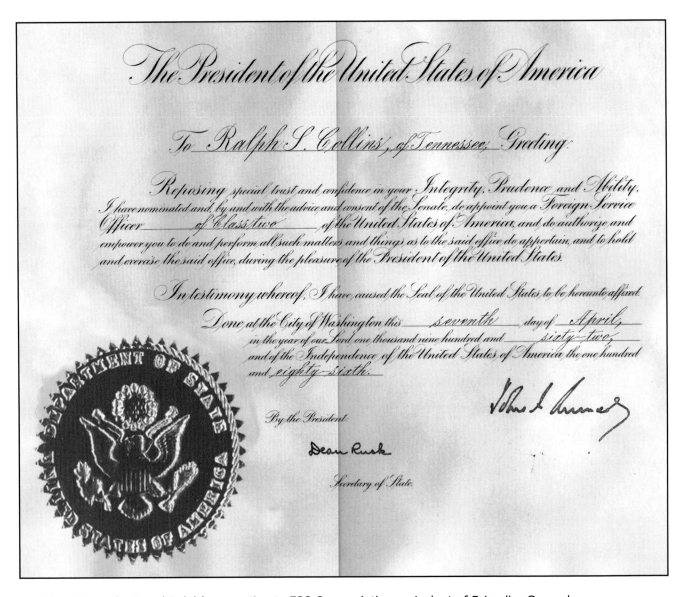

The President of the United States of America

To Ralph S. Collins, of Tennessee, Greeting:

Reposing special trust and confidence in your Integrity, Prudence and Ability, I have nominated and, by and with the advice and consent of the Senate, do appoint you a Foreign Service Officer of Class two of the United States of America, and do authorize and empower you to do and perform all such matters and things as to the said office do appertain, and to hold and exercise the said office, during the pleasure of the President of the United States.

In testimony whereof, I have caused the Seal of the United States to be hereunto affixed. Done at the City of Washington this seventh day of April, in the year of our Lord one thousand nine hundred and sixty-two, and of the Independence of the United States of America the one hundred and eighty-sixth.

By the President:

Dean Rusk

Secretary of State

President Kennedy signed Ralph's promotion to FSO-2, a rank the equivalent of Brigadier General.

Among our foreign friends in Montevideo were the Swedish Ambassador Hedengren and his French wife. We had many dinners together and enjoyed their company. Also, we had good friends in the Brazilian Embassy.

Among the new members of our Embassy were Eugene Boster, George Thigpen, and Richard Bloomfield. Dick's wife died, and he later remarried, and he became Ambassador to Portugal. Another fine officer at the Embassy was Bill McDonough. Others were Ned Holman, Ralph Visbal, Reuben Thomas, Fred Royt, Bill McLean, and James Willis (in my office).

My secretary, Bunnie Cannamela, was transferred to Asunción, where we visited her in August 1963. On our visit, Mary and I went to Iguassú Falls, and we stayed at a hotel on the Argentine side. Bunnie married a Paraguayan dentist, and they live now in New Jersey.

The best thing that happened to me in Uruguay was my promotion to FSO-2 in April 1962. To those unfamiliar with FSO ranks, that is the diplomatic equivalent of Brigadier General. Above it are the ranks of FSO-1 and Career Ambassador. Although I entered the Foreign Service at the advanced age of 35, I think I did quite well.

Western section of Great Smoky Mountains National Park, with Maryville to the northwest.

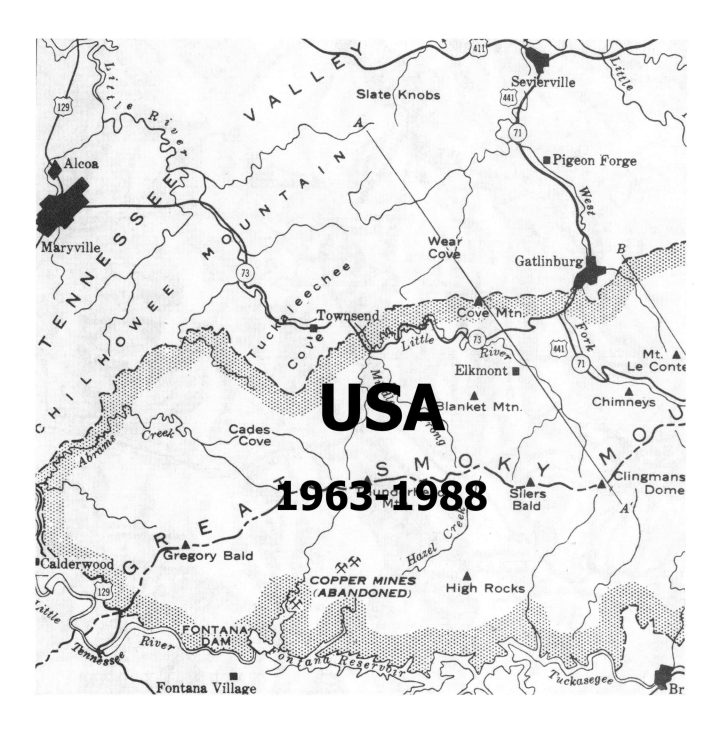

Slate Knobs

Sevierville

Pigeon Forge

Alcoa

Maryville

Wear Cove

Gatlinburg

Townsend

Tuckaleechee Cove

Cove Mtn.

Elkmont

USA

Mt. Le Conte

Blanket Mtn.

Chimneys

Cades Cove

1963-1988

Silers Bald

Clingmans Dome

Gregory Bald

Calderwood

COPPER MINES (ABANDONED)

High Rocks

FONTANA DAM

Fontana Village

Fontana Reservoir

Tuckasegee

Erica in front of the house on Nebraska Avenue in 2005.

Assignment: Washington

In October 1963 I was transferred to the State Department, where I had the title of Professor on the faculty of the Foreign Service Institute.

I lectured on Latin America in the National Interdepartmental Seminar. This Seminar had been set up in connection with the counter-insurgency effort that grew up as a result of various insurgent movements throughout the world, but especially in Latin America.

Attendance at the Seminar was required for senior-level officers of the Foreign Service (State Department), USIA, Agency for International Development (AID), Central Intelligence, and Military Attachés before they left on their foreign assignments.

The course lasted four weeks and consisted of lectures, discussion groups, both by subject and by area. The speakers included high-level government officials from the various departments.

We had such officials as Averill Harriman, Robert Kennedy, Robert McNamara, to name just a few. At the end of the third week, the Seminar students and many of the faculty flew down to Hurlburt Field (now Eglin Air Force Base) in Florida to attend military demonstrations and lectures. The next day the group stopped at Fort Bragg, North Carolina, to see the demonstrations of the Special Service troops.

When we returned to the States in the fall of 1963, Mother and I lived with Granny and Grandpa in Cornwall until Mother could find a house for us in Washington, DC.

I entered 8th grade, having skipped 7th, because I excelled on the proficiency test.

On November 22, 1963, an announcement was made over the loudspeaker at Cornwall Central High School saying President Kennedy had been shot. Everyone was sent home.

I walked back to Granny and Grandpa's house. We were all very upset and Grandpa did his best to explain to me what had happened.

Both Granny and Grandpa were a tremendous comfort to me during that time, when we watched all the latest news of the tragedy on television.

Melissa

Ralph, Maria Zubiller, Mary, Maria holding Chinela, and Melissa.

In the early years of the space exploration program there was one time when Mother was very excited about the new advances being made and spoke about it at the dinner table.

As a teenager, I wasn't interested in space programs or who was orbiting the earth. I was much more interested in the latest Rock and Roll craze from England: The Beatles.

Melissa

It was during my first Seminar in November 1963 that President Kennedy was killed in Dallas. I heard about it as I returned to the Seminar after lunch. The Seminar was suspended for a few days.

My duties at the Seminar included coordinating the lectures and briefings of all the Seminar students who were being assigned to Latin American posts. I had chief responsibility for that area, but I had to coordinate with representatives of the other agencies on the faculty.

It took a while to find a house, so Maria and Melissa did not join me immediately.

Eventually we then settled down at 5253 Nebraska Avenue, NW, a block off Connecticut Avenue. It was a pleasant house with a small backyard and an alley behind the house.

It was very convenient for me to catch a bus on Connecticut Avenue, which took me directly to the State Department. Melissa attended Woodrow Wilson High School.

I was encouraged to do some research while on this assignment. Among the papers I wrote:

"Age of Insurgency"

"U.S. Problems in Latin America"

"Communism in Latin America"

"The Mexican Revolution"

"Venezuela"

"The Sino-Soviet Rift and Latin America"

The family visited Kennedy's grave in Arlington National Cemetery.

October 6, 1964

AFFIDAVIT OF SUPPORT

I, RALPH STOKES COLLINS, a citizen of the United States, hereby declare my desire to sponsor the application for admission to the United Sates of visa applicant, MARIA PRICHELUSKI, at present resident in Montevideo, Uruguay.

During our residence in Montevideo from July, 1960 to September, 1963, Maria Pricheluski worked for us in the performance of general household work and as a companion to our daughter. We feel closely attached to Maria Pricheluski and it is our intention when she comes to the United States, to have her live with us in our home and to furnish her all basic necessities. We will also pay her wages of at least $50 a month and help her with extra wages working for other people. In no case will we allow her to become a public charge.

I am a Foreign Service Officer, employed by the US Department of State, Washington, DC. My annual income is at present $19,565. I support a family consisting of my wife and two daughters. I have no outstanding debts or other extraordinary financial obligations. I shall pay for the travel of Maria Pricheluski to the United States, meet her when she arrives, and receive her into our home for residence.

Ralph S. Collins   *Maria Zubiella Collins*

Once we children left home, we were on our own. No more financial support from Mom and Dad!

In this Affidavit of Support for the visa application of Maria Pricheluski, Dad says that he is supporting a wife and two daughters.

By this time I was 24 and Randall was 23, and we were on our own.

Erica

While living in Washington, the Collins family attended the Church of the Pilgrims.

I don't know that I uncovered anything new or brilliant, but I was rather proud of the last one, because the rift between the Soviet Union and China at that time revolved to a great extent around the Chinese Communist criticism of the Soviet leadership for its lack of will in Latin America, especially at the time of the Cuban missile crisis.

I went on so many of the trips to Hurlburt Field and Fort Bragg that I began to skip the night maneuvers at Hurlburt and to spend the evening at the Holiday Inn in Fort Walton Beach, where we always stayed.

There were two special trips to Latin America during my four years at the Institute. In December 1964 I took a trip to Venezuela, Panamá, and Guatemala.

I spent five days in Caracas, talking to Embassy officers and doing some sightseeing. Paul Frantz from the Institute went with me. We flew to Panamá, where we spent another six days attending a regional conference, and we had plenty of time to visit US military installations and the Panama Canal.

I then traveled alone to Guatemala, where I spent several days with the Mitchells, who had been with me in Montevideo. I got in a nice excursion to Antigua while I was in Guatemala.

The other special trip was in January 1967. I visited Barbados (which I had seen before on a trip up from Uruguay), spent several days in Georgetown (in Guyana), a couple of days in Trinidad, then in Santo Domingo (Dominican Republic), Port-au-Prince (Haiti), and Kingston (Jamaica).

USAF plane at Hurlburt Field.

Ralph in tuxedo with guests at the Collins home.

The National Interdepartmental Seminar taught senior officials from many branches of government, both civilian and military, about counter-insurgency on the world scene.

Ralph represented the State Department on insurgency in Latin America. Ralph also mentions frequent visits during this period to Fort Bragg, North Carolina, the major US military center for counter-insurgency.

Randall

The Deputy Chief of Mission in Kingston had taken our Seminar before going to Jamaica, and he invited me to stay at his home up in the mountains while I was there.

The faculty of the National Interdepartmental Seminar in 1967:

Ambassador Randolph A. Kidder, Coordinator

Gordon H. Mattison, Deputy Coordinator

Captain Lee Blocker, US Navy, Defense Dept.

Ralph S. Collins, Department of State

Donald Q. Coster, AID

Daniel L. Horowitz, Department of State

Andrew J. Kaufman, Department of State

Joseph M. Ludlow, Department of State

Justin E. O'Donnell, Department of Defense

Gerald M. Strauss, AID

Spencer L. Taggart, Department of Defense

Washington during the years 1963-67 was full of our Foreign Service friends. We saw Ambassador and Mrs. Woodward frequently. Our dear friends the Pratts were there part of the time. To enumerate or mention everyone would tax my memory, but they were a great joy to us.

In June 1964 we attended Erica's wedding to Carl Ellenberger in Rochester, New York, and then we embarked on a five-week trip to California with Mary and Melissa.

My admiration for Dad's facility in six languages sparked my courage to take courses in four languages at once during my junior year in college: French, German, Russian, plus an independent study in Spanish.

And then, of course, I was able eventually to have a career as a professor of French and Spanish.

Mary

Maria and Ralph in 1965.

Maria and Ralph with Mary in Baton Rouge at Mary's graduation from LSU, in 1965.

We stopped to see Hill Shine in Kentucky, we visited the Barricks (from Maryville College) and Gassers (from Berlin) in Las Cruces, New Mexico; and we stayed a few days with the Prisbecks in Tucson and with the Livorneses in Nogales.

We visited the Grand Canyon, Bryce Canyon, and Zion National Park, left Las Vegas way before daybreak to avoid the heat in the desert and arrived at Disneyland in time to be the first ones in. We spent a night in Los Angeles and went on up the coast to San Francisco and Berkeley.

We spent a week in Berkeley near Randall and Bryson's apartment. From there we visited San Francisco, Palo Alto (Stanford), Yosemite, and Sequoia, and then we went up the California and Oregon coast to Seattle. There we visited Dr. Paul Tueffers, whom we had met in Regensburg in 1951, when he was a student.

We returned East via Yellowstone, Cody, Black Hills, Wisconsin, Ann Arbor, Detroit, and Niagara Falls, to Cornwall-on-Hudson. Thus I used up some of my accumulated home leave from the Foreign Service.

In 1965 we went down to Baton Rouge for Mary's graduation from LSU. We returned by way of the Gulf Coast, Saint Augustine, and Charleston, stopping in Ayden, before returning to Washington.

In 1967 Mary got her MA from Columbia University. She continued graduate work there and took a job at Allegheny College in 1968. While at Columbia she stayed at International House on Riverside Drive.

Christmas in Cornwall-on-Hudson. From left: Ralph, Melissa, Mary, friend, Erica, friend, Maria and Alfred Zubiller.

In the last year of their residence in Washington, Mother took a job with the US Census Bureau as a census taker.

Because information needed to be gathered on a regular basis, she visited people in their homes with lists of questions to ask.

Mother enjoyed finding the addresses and interviewing people. Financially, this gave her her own nest egg, which she invested wisely when she arrived in Maryville.

Mary

At the end of May 1967, I had a double hernia operation at Georgetown Hospital. While I was in the hospital, my oldest brother John Arthur died in Ayden. I was unable to go to the funeral, but Maria went. I was saddened by his death, because Arthur and his wife had been almost like parents to me after my parents died.

While recuperating from my operation, I visited Maryville. I had been in correspondence with the College since December of 1966, and they offered me a job as Chairman of the Foreign Language Department.

Because I saw no immediate opportunity for another foreign assignment in the Foreign Service, I resigned July 3, 1967, effective August 31.

Because the house we were renting on Nebraska Avenue had been sold, we had to move out by August 1. Young Larry Kirwan came down from Cornwall to help Maria bring our furniture down to Maryville. They got it installed it in our house at 1741 Linda Lane, which I had purchased earlier in the summer.

I was able to live in Bob and Grace Hayes' house in Bethesda, Maryland, while the Hayes were at their summer place on Cape Cod for the month of August, until I finished my Washington assignment.

On August 26 Maria and I returned to Maryville. Two days later, my younger brother Jack died in Ayden. I attended the funeral. It was the third brother I had lost in 18 months!

Department of State

UNITED STATES OF AMERICA

to Ralph S. Collins

on your retirement from the Foreign Service it is my privilege to express to you the appreciation of the Government of the United States for the

Loyal and Meritorious Service

which you have rendered your country
In your career of 22 years devoted to the interests of the American people you have earned the gratitude and respect of your Government.

Done at the city of Washington this 31st day of August In the year of Our Lord One Thousand Nine Hundred and Sixty-Seven

Dean Rusk
Secretary of State

324

After losing 3 brothers to heart attacks I decided to stay active and resolved to walk and take care of the yard once we got settled in Maryville.

My move back into the academic world was really a gradual one. First, my assignment at the Foreign Service Institute was with the title of Professor, so I was actually doing some teaching in addition to researching and writing papers.

At the end of December 1964, the Modern Language Association (MLA) held its annual meeting in New York. Because we were spending Christmas in Cornwall-on-Hudson with Alfred and Maria Zubiller, Maria's parents, I went down to the city to attend an MLA session.

Then again in 1966, when the MLA met in Washington, I attended some of the sessions. I began renewing some of my memberships – to the MLA, the South Atlantic Modern Language Association, and the American Association of Teachers of German.

After getting back into teaching at Maryville, I joined other organizations, such as the Mountain Interstate Foreign Language Conference. These were some of the moves in resuming an academic career after 22 years in the Foreign Service.

View from the front of Maria and Ralph's house, with the Smoky Mountains on the horizon.

Returning to Maryville, Tennessee

With all our moving around, we had never owned our home. In the early days in Maryville, 1935-45, we could not afford to buy a house. So the house at 1741 Linda Lane, into which we moved in August 1967, is the only home we have owned.

Of course, with all the children married, it is large for two people, but good for visits by children and grandchildren. We had the small back patio built up into a back porch, screened in for the summer, with plastic panels for the winter. We have also had all the extra insulation put in according to the TVA recommendations.

Returning to Maryville was a return home and the renewal of friendships and associations from the previous period. Our friends among the newcomers to Maryville are amazed at the number of people we know here.

Joseph Copeland, whom we had met in 1961, when we were on home leave from Montevideo, was President of the College. I taught full-time and served as Head of the Foreign Language Department in 1967-77. Thereafter I taught a couple of years, part-time, mainly German.

In 1967 I taught French literature and Spanish, in addition to German. At the beginning, we were still in the post-Sputnik period of emphasis on foreign languages, and the enrollment at Maryville College was high, heading toward the 1,000 mark.

Above: Thaw Hall, the Maryville College library.
Below: Anderson Hall, in the center of campus.

When I was a little boy, Grandpa took me for walks on the Maryville campus and in the College Woods. There he taught me about the trees and flowers and where the streams flowed.

Afterwards we always stopped at Isaac Student Union for a cream soda. I still like cream sodas to this day!

Chris Mann

By 1977 this trend had slackened and the foreign-language requirement was abandoned. After I retired in 1977, the Foreign Language Department came eventually to be under the English Department.

Boyd Daniels was Dean of the College in 1967-69. Then Malcolm Willey, a very good friend and Professor of Sociology, was Acting Executive Officer. He died in 1974, and Carolyn Blair became Dean. In 1978, when Dr. Wayne Anderson became President, Dr. Alfred Perkins became Academic Vice-President (Dean).

In 1967-68 the Foreign Language Department members were: Catherine Wilkinson, French (1919-69!); Richard Fridenbergs, French, German, Russian (1961-68); Kathryn Martin, Spanish, French, (1950-87); Howard Schwam, Spanish, (1947-70); Arthur Dees, German (1965-68); and Grace Rodriguez, Spanish (1967-75).

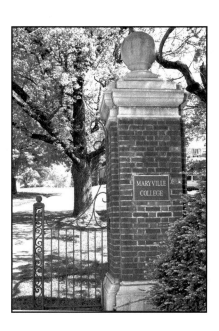

Roland Lukner came in 1968 and taught German and Russian until 1972, when he returned to Germany. Naomi Lesko came in 1968 and taught French until 1970. Marie-Ange Meyer-Plate came in 1969 and taught French until 1971, when her husband was transferred back to Germany. Marja Hanson, French, came in 1972 and left in 1975 to go to the College of Charleston.

I was very lucky in my return to college teaching. It just happened that the primary need the first year (1967-68) was for someone in French, so most all my classes were French. My enthusiasm and that of my students seems to have been concentrated in French 311 and 312, survey courses in French literature.

Maria and Ralph in the study at their home at 1741 Linda Lane,
the only house they ever owned.

The text I used was Bishop's two-volume *A Survey of French Literature*. We had a lively class and a good spirit. I remember some of the best students very well: Edwin Best, Jr., Susan Carr, Barbara Jean Griffith, Linda McNair, Susan Fershee, Marilyn Martin, Kathrine Munson, and Dee Snyder.

Dee was blind – I'll never forget the day when she asked me in good French if she could recite one of the Ronsard poems we had been studying. She did it so beautifully that we were all delighted. It was an inspiring experience.

The second year (1968-69) I taught only German, due to the retirement of Mr. Fridenbergs and the departure of Arthur Dees, both of whom had taught German. Again I had one of my best German students, Susan Fershee, and the next year (1969-70) I had Linda Coyner, Marilyn Martin, and Steve Horning.

After graduating, Steve studied for a year at Marburg, became an information officer with USIA, and was assigned to Katmandu, Nepal. I believe he later went to a Seminary and entered the ministry. Susan Fershee went on to do post-graduate work. Later I had William Postler, Betsey Joyner, and Angela Peterson. These were some of my best students. Beginning in 1974, I also taught some Spanish classes.

The structure of courses at Maryville had changed considerably since I had left in 1945. Between Thanksgiving and Christmas, there was the so-called Interim session, during which the students took a special course.

A multi-lingual feast

During Dad's sabbatical leave in 1973, we visited relatives in Germany, various friends from the foreign service, and former students of Dad's.

The most memorable visit for me was with Jean-Claude Lebouteiller, who had been on the faculty of the French Department at Allegheny College, where Mary and Lou taught. We met up with him in Arcachon, and he then joined us on our trip to Spain.

In Madrid Jean-Claude invited two Spanish girls to join us for dinner. They spoke no English, so they spoke in Spanish. Jean-Claude spoke no Spanish, so he spoke in English or French. I babbled in English, French, or Spanish, depending on the person I was talking to.

It was the most amazing conversation: three languages, and we could speak in whichever we wanted and still understand the gist of the conversation! And if we really had trouble with a word, we just asked Dad to translate, as he was fluent in all three!

Erica

Ralph at the Parthenon in Athens, Greece.

It could be entirely different from one's major and would quite likely involve off-campus projects. The first two years, I chose subjects from my Foreign Service experience: in 1967, "Problems of the Developing Nations," and in 1968, "Problems of Latin America."

In 1969 my subject was "Faust in English." In 1970 I organized a trip to Mexico for a small group of Spanish majors. We travelled to Mexico City, Cuernavaca, Acapulco, Taxco, Pátzcuaro, Guadalajara, Guanajuato, and Monterrey. Among the group was our daughter Melissa, who enjoyed being back in a Spanish-speaking environment.

In 1971 I managed to join an Interim group that went to Greece. After a few days in London, where we visited the Greek sculptures at the British Museum, we flew to Athens. We had a grand time visiting islands, including Crete and Rhodes, and we took a bus trip through the Pelopónnisos; Mycenae, Sparta, Olympia, and Delphi. It was the fulfillment of one of my dreams, namely to visit the Classical places. We made a stop-over in Lisbon on the way home.

In 1972 my Interim course was "The Greening of Hermann Hesse." As Hesse was very popular among students in those days, the course was a great success. In 1974 my Interim came up-to-date with Heinrich Böll as the subject. In 1975 my Interim was "The Russian's World."

In the fall of 1973 I took a Sabbatical trip to Europe. My daughter Erica accompanied me. We left New York October 2 and returned November 16. We flew KLM and landed in Amsterdam.

Ralph and Melissa at her graduation from Maryville College, 1972.

Our itinerary included Köln, Frankfurt, Heidelberg, Munich, Vienna, Linz, Salzburg, Innsbruck, Konstanz, Zürich, Bern, Basel, Luzern, Lausanne, Dijon, Paris, Arcachon, Bilbao, Santiago, Salamanca, Madrid, Barcelona, Avignon, Marseille, Geneva, Strasbourg, and Amsterdam.

We travelled by train, with Eurail-Pass. This made it easy to get around, because everything in Europe is well served by good, fast trains.

We found the Eurail-Pass very useful for another reason. We had trouble finding hotel accommodations in the big cities – Munich, Vienna, and Zürich. In the case of Vienna, we merely used Linz as our hotel-city and returned each day to Vienna for our sight-seeing. Furthermore, Linz is important for Anton Bruckner.

In the case of Zürich, after inquiring about hotels, we wasted no time looking further, and toward evening we took a train to Olten, well-situated as to train connections. We used it as our hotel-base for trips to Neuchâtel and Bern.

On a Saturday morning we went from Olten to Basel, where we visited the zoo, and returned to Olten to take a half-hour train ride to Zürich to attend the Opera, returning to Olten at midnight.

From Lausanne we went to Leysin, above Montreux and stayed with a former Maryville professor, Art Ainsworth. We stopped in Dijon on the way to Paris to deliver a wedding present from Mary to a German instructor at Allegheny College who had married a French girl. In Paris we stayed at

Ralph and the Spanish Honor Society, 1970.

335

Governor Lamar Alexander with Maria and Ralph on a visit to Maryville.

an old hotel recommended by Art Ainsworth, Grand
Hotel Oriental. It was not very grand but it was
comfortable. While in Paris we were entertained by
Ambassador Kidder (FSI), who had a place
overlooking the Senate (Luxembourg Gardens).

Another night a friend from Berlin days (1947),
Bernard Bonnafous, took us out to dinner at one of
the highly rated restaurants of Paris. Bernard lived on
Avenue Roosevelt, just off the Champs-Elysées.

We took a very fast train from Paris to
Bordeaux – it just whizzed through the countryside at
more than 100 miles per hour. We were supposed to
meet Jean-Claude Lebouteiller, a friend of Mary and
Lou, whom I had met at Allegheny when he was a
visiting professor.

Although he had not received our card saying
we would be there on Sunday instead of Saturday, he
picked us up at the station and took us to Arcachon,
where he was professor in a school.

Ralph's first grandchild, Randall's
daughter Lindsay, in 1967.

It was a beautiful, sunny afternoon and the bay
was full of colorful sailing boats. Sailing was one of
Jean-Claude's hobbies. It so happened that the school
had a week of holiday, so we invited Jean-Claude to
go with us to Spain, and he accepted.

We stopped for a couple of nights in Bilbao,
where we visited old haunts and Spanish friends,
having dinner in Las Arenas. Our main goal in Spain
was Santiago de Compostela, the object of European
pilgrimages in the Middle Ages.

While Consul at Bilbao, I had planned to visit
Santiago, but something always interfered. We made it

I was thrilled to take Dad up on his invitation to join him for a six-week trip to Europe during his sabbatical leave.

I had not been abroad since 1960! This was my one opportunity during my 17-year first marriage to visit the countries where I had grown up.

Dad and I visited Germany, Austria, Switzerland, France, and Spain, and to please me, he made up the itinerary with special emphasis on music.

We visited Mozart's house, where I saw the original of the fortepiano that Carl was building for me, and we attended many concerts, including one at St. Florian, the church near Linz where Bruckner had played the organ.

Erica

this time and celebrated my 63rd birthday at the Hostal de los Reyes Católicos. We then went to Madrid via Salamanca, where Jean-Claude had friends. From there, Jean-Claude returned to Arcachon and we went on to Barcelona and then to France, staying a few nights in Avignon and making trips to Aix-en-Provence and Marseille.

Then we went to Geneva and Strasbourg. The third night in Germany, we went to visit our German relatives in Dörnbach. Erich took us to a dance in Rockenhausen, and Sunday we all went to the opera in Kaiserslautern. On the return from Strasbourg, we again visited uncles, aunts, and cousins for a few days. Then we took a train to Amsterdam, where we were able to attend an orchestra concert at the Konzertgebouw, the famous music hall. From Amsterdam we flew back to New York. Erica returned to her house in Mt. Gretna, Pennsylvania, and I went back to Maryville. It had been a great trip for both of us.

In June of 1976 I went with Erica and Carl to the Rocky Mountain National Park for about 10 days of hiking. On one of these hikes, Erica asked me why I didn't join a hiking club since I was going to retire from full-time teaching. I thought that was a good idea, and I have been doing a lot of hiking ever since, especially in the Smokies.

In the fall of 1976 I went on another college Interim trip, this time "In Search of King Arthur." We spent about a week in London, during which time we visited Canterbury and Cambridge. Then we went on a bus trip to Oxford, Stratford-on-Avon, Coventry,

Canterbury Cathedral.

Grandsons Alan and Adrian, August 1974.

Apple harvest from tree in backyard at Linda Lane.

Our sons, Adrian and Alan, received a wonderful education in the summers as they were growing up. They visited Mother and Dad in Tennessee for a month or so. They learned oil painting, macramé, cooking, hiking, biking, gardening, and how to entertain guests and be sociable.

They went to Nashville to meet Governor Lamar Alexander at his office and to Ghost Ranch in New Mexico, where they learned to use water colors to record the desert landscape.

Mary

Wells, Cornwall, Winchester, and so on. It was very cold in some hotels, but we enjoyed the trip very much. I would like to go again, perhaps in the summer time.

In addition to my teaching, I attended a lot of meetings of organizations having to do with foreign languages: the Southern Conference on Language Teaching; the South Atlantic Modern Language Association; and the Mountain Interstate Foreign Language Conference.

At Easter time every year from 1968 to 1975, I attended the University of Kentucky Foreign Language Conference. That allowed me to visit my friend Hill Shine, who taught at Kentucky after the war and then retired to his old colonial cottage on Tates' Creek Road.

One year Mary and Louis attended this conference. In 1972 we heard Dr. Urban T. Holmes, my former professor at the University of North Carolina, give one of his last papers before he died. From 1968 to 1974 I attended all the meetings of the Tennessee Philological Society. After I retired from full-time teaching in 1977, I slacked off, and gradually quit attending these meetings.

My part-time teaching continued for a few years. In 1977-78 I taught five classes of French, one of Spanish, and three of German. Actually that was a full load. In 1978-79 I taught two classes of German and one of French, and in 1980-81 I taught two classes of German. I have not taught a class since the winter of 1981.

New Providence Presbyterian Church photo in 1976.

Ralph and his hiking companions: Margaret Stevenson beside Ralph on the log; Elgin Kintner, Lorene Smith, and David Smith standing in the rear.

Staying active in retirement

Retirement has meant a lot of hiking in the Great Smokies and the Appalachian Trail south of the Smokies, down to Springer Mountain in Georgia. For a few years I hiked as much as 2,000 miles a year. Now I average almost 100 miles a month.

The longest hike I have taken was 32 miles: from Clingman's Dome to Fontana. The last hour of that was in the dark, and I shall not plan to hike that much again. It is good exercise, and I feel good hiking this much. It is also enjoyable from the standpoint of beautiful views, flowers, and animals. I hope I can keep it up.

Retirement also means trying to keep up with the grandchildren. Mary's twins, Adrian and Alan, have spent every Christmas with us since they were born in October, 1970, and they have also visited us every summer.

Randy's three children have been to see us: Lindsay, born in 1966; Anthony, in 1975; and Maren Diane, in 1977. Lindsay will graduate from Pomona College this year (1988). Melissa's son, Christopher, was born in November, 1984.

Maria's mother came to live with us in 1973. She is now in a nursing home. Maria has been very active in community organizations of all sorts. I take a back seat in such things. I did join Kiwanis several years ago and take an active interest in the programs. I play golf twice a week when the weather permits.

Ralph's genealogy research was impressive, and he spent hours explaining to me how he did it and where to find the resources.

One afternoon when Erica and I were visiting in Maryville, he took me to meet his friend and hiking partner, Dr. Elgin Kintner, who was doing his family history.

Elgin showed me a copy of an old map of western Pennsylvania on which the farm of his ancestor was named.

Right next to it was a farm that belonged to one of my ancestors. I was hooked! Ralph and Elgin launched me on my own genealogy trek.

Bill Steffee (Ralph's son-in-law)

When I was 11, I started spending a few weeks each summer in Maryville with Nana and Manga (Maria and Ralph). One of my strongest memories is of Nana's pies. She sent me out to pick gooseberries from the yard. I tasted a raw one from the bush and couldn't imagine that it could turn into something I would want to eat. . .but it did!

Another time, when Manga and I were hiking in the Smoky Mountains, we found wild blueberries. We filled up one of our empty water bottles with the tiny things and brought them home to Nana. The next day we had delicious wild blueberry pie with lunch!

Lindsay Olesberg

A few years ago I got interested in tracing the family history. I spent some time in Eastern North Carolina looking up records and visiting my two sisters, Estelle and Rosa. With a lot of luck, I have been able to trace some lines back into the 1600s.

I have found nothing startling or earth-shaking, but I did find at least one ancestor, Daniel Venters, who participated in the Revolutionary War and may have lost his life in it. As he is not listed in Sons of the American Revolution (SAR) or elsewhere, I sent his information off to them. Although I didn't have as much documentation as I would have liked, I was accepted for membership in the SAR!

In April 1982 I received a call from Mary asking if I could come up to Allegheny College to finish out the term for two German professors. They had both had major surgery and were unable to teach for the remainder of the school year. I agreed to do it and drove up to Meadville, where I taught a class a day – all at the intermediate level – for 6 days a week.

Adrian and Duffy.

I enjoyed spending time with my grandsons, Alan and Adrian. We threw baseballs in the yard, went exploring in the woods, mowed the huge lawn, and played with Erica's samoyed, Duffy, who was staying at the Wagner's house while she was out of town.

One Sunday while we were at church, Duffy got two packages of ground meat off the kitchen counter (way back by the wall) where Mary had put them for thawing. When we arrived he had already eaten one package, styrofoam and all. We learned not to underestimate his ability to get things!

Charlie's Bunion.

Hiking up LeConte and other trails

One of the most exhilarating hikes I ever took with Dad was to the top of Mt. LeConte. He did this hike on a regular basis, over 100 times as he kept count.

Lou and I went up with him just once, and that was when we were in our 40s! We stayed overnight at the Lodge atop the mountain in the fog with black bears roaming around.

It was on that hike that I realized that five miles downhill is just as strenuous as five miles uphill, especially in a drizzle on a slippery trail.

Mary

Ralph and Erica in an abandoned car in the Tremont area of the Smoky Mountains.

Dad loved to hike! Whenever I visited Tennessee, he took me on a hike, usually in the Smoky Mountains, but also on the Greenbelt in Maryville or around his neighborhood on the west side of the city. Whenever I return to Maryville, I feel an urge to get outside and go for a long walk!

Erica

Above: LeConte on the horizon.
Below: Margaret, Elgin, and Ralph.

Ralph explains the trails to student hikers from France and Germany.

Ralph returning from a winter hike to Spence Field in 1987.

I have had many fine hiking friends and companions. My first hike with Margaret Stevenson and Elgin Kintner happened to be the last trail they had not yet hiked in the Great Smokies – a goal which I have not achieved and probably will not. I have hiked all the Park trails on the Tennessee side.

The second hike was with Margaret Stevenson and some Knoxville hikers who came over regularly to hike with Margaret – Phil and Ruth Ewald and Elsie Dodson.

Eventually I hiked with many other local hikers. Elgin Kintner led us on many interesting hikes, some of them quite long and some off-trail. More recently, two of the most devoted hikers have been Lorene Smith, who gave me good advice and encouragement in the genealogical research, and Shirley Henry.

Our favorite hikes include all four trails up Mt. Le Conte as well as Spence Field, Gregory Bald, Hangover, Slickrock Creek, Abrams Falls, Cove Mountain, Rich Mountain, and many others. Les Webb and I have hiked together many times, especially in late July to Gregory Bald to pick blueberries. Several years ago Les fought a bear which had seized his knapsack. Les was victorious.

In 1987 I hiked up Le Conte for the 100th time. It is my favorite hike, and I hope to continue hiking it for a long time. In fact, I like the symbolism of conquering mountains.

Maryville today, with Linda Lane in lower left.

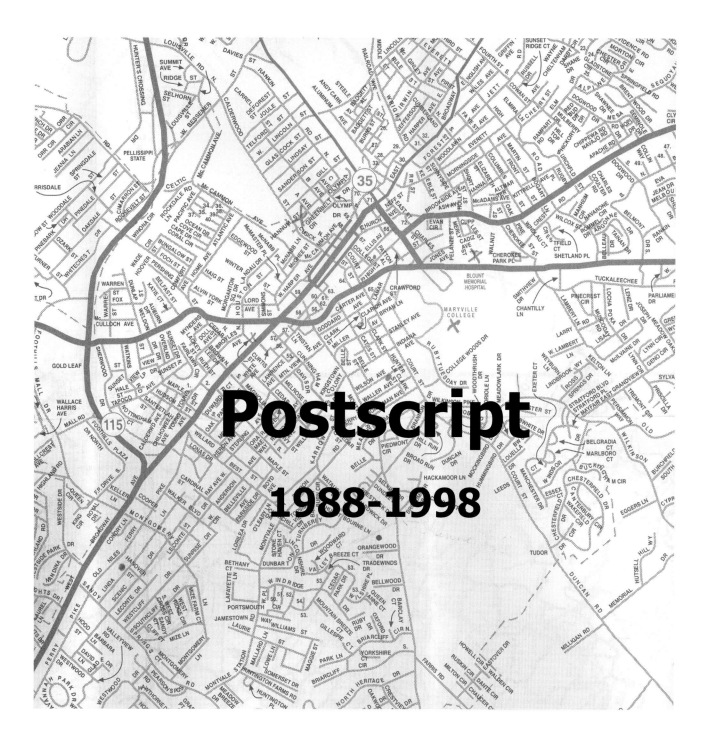

Postscript
1988-1998

Randy's wife, Judy McConnell, Anthony, and Maren present a globe to Ralph and Maria, with pins to indicate all the places where members of the family had lived.

Ralph and Maria cut their 50th anniversary cake as Lindsay and Chris watch.

Ralph presents *View from LeConte* to the family at the 50th anniversary dinner.

Postscript

On August 17, 1988, the family gathered at Sawmill Creek Resort in Huron, Ohio, to celebrate Mother and Dad's 50th wedding anniversary. Dad distributed copies of *View from LeConte* to his children and grandchildren, along with the genealogy compilation he had prepared after many years of research: *Our Collins-Ives-Stokes-Venters-Hartsfield Family*.

He played golf and took walks with us, rode rides with his grandkids at Cedar Point Amusement Park, and spent a lot of time reminiscing as the family pored through his memoirs and the photo albums that Mother had prepared for each of their four children.

Randy and his family presented Mother and Dad with a globe covered with pins of different colors representing where they and their children and grandchildren had lived and traveled. At a time when travel abroad was infrequent, our family had traveled a lot!

Back in Maryville he resumed a busy schedule of playing golf with friends at the Green Meadow Country Club, going to weekly Kiwanis meetings, and attending church services and weekly dinners at New Providence Presbyterian Church.

Mother and Dad belonged to this church from their earliest days in Maryville in the late 1930's. Even though they traveled abroad for some 20 years, they always stayed members of this church.

Maria and Ralph at the first Collins reunion, in 1992, which Maria helped organize.

Ralph telling stories of early days in North Carolina to Melissa and nephew Jack Collins.

On a visit to Lake Louise, Ralph and Maria took Erica and me on a hike to Lake Agnes. Maria and I set out at a slow, steady pace with frequent stops to rest.

Ralph in the meantime raced up the trail, hiked back down to see how we were doing, and took off again. Back and forth he went as we hiked the one-mile trail, covering a far greater distance than we.

Bill Steffee

Hike to Lake Agnes in 1989: Ralph, Maria, Lou, and Mary.

Dad kept up his knowledge of foreign languages by alternately reading for a week in one or another of the languages he knew best: German, Spanish, French, Italian, and Russian. He even took classes in Japanese at Maryville College!

Mother and Dad had a large circle of friends whom they saw regularly, whether at church, at home, at bridge games, at meetings of one sort or another, or on the hiking trails.

Mother and Dad continued to travel. In the fall of 1987 they took a trip to Germany with their close friends, Julie and Norton Rop and Marilyn and Warren Stritter. The next year they traveled to Banff and Jasper in the Canadian Rockies with Erica and Bill, meeting up with Mary and Lou en route. In 1990 they took a trip to Alaska with Aunt Emma Toepert. They attended Lindsay's wedding to Jon Olesberg in April 1991.

When Mary's twin sons graduated from different colleges on the same day in June 1992, Dad attended Adrian's graduation from Allegheny College while Mother attended Alan's graduation from Pomona College.

Back in Tennessee, Dad's new passion became hiking. He hiked in the Smoky Mountains several times a week, trying different trails, or looking for ripe berries, or admiring the spring wild flowers. There was something to see every season of the year.

Whenever Bill and I visited Maryville, he took us for a hike in the mountains. We made it a point to visit each year in April in order to see the wild flowers

Maria Collins heads up the residential campaign which is now over 107 percent of goal. - Times Staff Photo by Michael Hughes

UW residential division volunteers exceed goal

The residential division of the United Way campaign has been especially successful this year, according to figures released through the Blount County United Way office.

Part of that success has come through the chairman of that division and the volunteers which have worked under her, United Way officials say.

Maria Collins has been in charge this year and the figure for the division now stands at 107.3 percent of goal.

Above: Maria with Mary and Alan at his graduation from Pomona College.
Right: Ralph at Adrian's graduation from Allegheny College with John Wagner, on the left, and Chris.

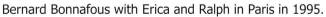

Bernard Bonnafous with Erica and Ralph in Paris in 1995.

in bloom. And we made a special trip to Maryville to accompany him on his 100th hike up Mt. LeConte!

When he wasn't hiking in the Smokies, Dad took long walks in his neighborhood – which wasn't as built up as it is now – past neighbors' houses and along the farmers' fields and pastures.

Or he drove into town, parked on the college campus, and walked the Greenbelt, stopping in at the county library to see friends and check up on genealogy questions, and spending time in the college library at the end of his walk reading the daily newspapers.

On November 4, 1992 Mother, Dad's life-long companion, with whom he had traveled so far and experienced so much, died of cancer. She was laid to rest in the Maryville College cemetery.

In 1996 Melissa and her son Chris moved into the house on Linda Lane to live with Dad. He continued to hike with friends, to walk the Greenbelt, and go to Sunday School and church services at New Providence Presbyterian.

Dad also did some more traveling, with Bill and me, including a trip to Japan in 1993 and a trip to France in 1995. While in Paris he had a wonderful reunion with his old friend from Berlin days, Bernard Bonnafous.

But it became apparent to family and friends that Dad was showing signs of dementia, and in February of 1998 we moved him to Judson Park Retirement Community in Cleveland. Judson was one block from our house and I visited him daily.

Right: At a Collins reunion in Maryville: Erica, Lou, Melissa, Ralph, Randall, Chris, Mary, Bill, and Adrian.

Below: Ralph crossing Abrams Creek above Cades Cove.

Dad adjusted easily, living in a room filled with familiar furniture and with certificates and photos on the walls. He participated in exercise and painting classes and went on field trips. He enjoyed listening to me play the piano and weekly conversations with a volunteer from Germany who conversed with him in German. Dad especially enjoyed visits by his children and grandchildren.

A few weeks after his 88th birthday, Dad suffered a massive stroke. He died on November 21, 1998. His funeral service was held in New Providence Church. He is buried beside Mother in the Maryville College cemetery.

In his last two decades Dad had continued to enjoy concerts and plays, friends and family. He reflected on his good fortune in being able to enjoy operas in Italy, ballets and plays in Moscow and Munich. He looked back with pride at his children's accomplishments, and he took pleasure in seeing his grandchildren mature.

He delighted in the hikes he took in the Great Smoky Mountains of Tennessee. It was Dad's love of the mountains and his pride in having scaled Mt. LeConte hundreds of times that led him to title his autobiography *View from LeConte*.

Erica Collins Steffee, 2008

Ralph with grandsons Alan, Adrian, Chris, and Anthony.

Ralph's granddaughter Lindsay with husband, John Olesberg, and Ralph's great-grandson Michael.

Ralph (center) and the Wagner men: Lou, Adrian, Alan, John.

Erica and Ralph dancing at the wedding of Laura Steffee and George Kozma, in Cleveland in December, 1993.

Japan: fulfillment of a dream

Dad had a very strong desire to visit Japan, fostered in part by Randy's sociology books being translated into Japanese as soon as they were published.

Dad took Japanese language classes at Maryville College and regularly helped a Japanese student with her reading of newspaper articles at the college library.

Bill's company had a branch in Tokyo, and he invited Dad and me to go along for a three-week visit in the fall of 1993.

Dad was thrilled! We were escorted on our trip by company staff members and saw a wide range of sights, from historic temples to peoples' homes. Dad said that the trip fulfilled a long-standing dream!

Erica

Dad really wanted to climb Mt. Fuji even though it was not the traditional climbing season.

I accompanied Dad, and we were the only ones on the trail! We got about two thirds of the way to the top, as I am showing in the picture above right, when clouds started to move in, and we felt it prudent to come back down.

Climbing on volcanic rock was quite a challenge!

Erica

Randall and Ralph in Cleveland in 1997.

In 1992 the University of California at Riverside presented me with an honorary award as the Faculty Research Lecturer. In the faculty procession we all wore academic caps and gowns, with colors representing our particular degrees and universities. It was an occasion to remember all the tradition in this institution.

It always makes me think of how the university as an organization goes back to the Middle Ages, because we still wear our university robes on these occasions.

Also, since I have studied the history of universities, it reminds me of how all modern universities go back to the reform which started in the German universities in the late 1800s, and how American scholars as late as Dad's generation went to study in Germany. There is a lot of historical continuity, and I feel that our family is part of that tradition.

Randy

Dad came over at 9 a.m. today. He had had his walk and wanted to get working on my back hedges.

After church we went to Townsend for dinner at a little place that serves a nice Southern-style Sunday buffet.

At 2:00 we went to Maryville College's commencement. It was a beautiful day so they held it outside. Afterward Dad, Chris, and I walked to the cemetery. The flowers on Mother's grave are doing fine.

Dad came over for dinner. I grilled some steaks outside and made a big salad.

As it was getting dark, Dad went home and Chris turned in for the night. Was I glad I didn't have any papers to grade today!

Letter from Melissa to Erica
May 15, 1993

Overstreet first recipient of Collins Professorship in the Humanities

By Karen Eldridge
Maryville College

During a luncheon and inaugural installation ceremony held recently in Maryville College's Proffitt Dining Room, Dr. Sam Overstreet was named the first professor of the college to hold the Dr. Ralph S. Collins Professorship in the Humanities.

Overstreet, a professor of English, earned his doctoral degree in medieval studies from Cornell University and his bachelor's degree from Yale. A member of Phi Beta Kappa and an active medieval textual scholar, his teaching interests lie in Chaucer, early Western literature and history of the English language. He joined the MC faculty in 1990.

"His 15 years on the faculty chronicle a great many notables," said Dr. Robert Naylor, vice president and dean, during the installation ceremony. "His peers have elected him to nearly every major committee of the faculty; he has served as chair of the faculty; the junior and senior classes have honored him for outstanding teaching; and he is a scholar of some renown."

Established by Collins' daughter and son-in-law, Erica Collins Steffe and William P. Steffe, the professorship memorializes Dr. Collins, who taught foreign languages at the College from 1935 until 1945 and again from 1967 until 1981. Bridging his teaching years at the College were 22 years as a foreign-service officer in Germany, the former Soviet Union, Spain, Italy and Uruguay. Prior to his return to the College in 1967, he was a member of the faculty of the State Department's Foreign Service Institute in Washington, D.C.

The professorship recognizes exemplary accomplishment as a teacher scholar and faculty member. The endowment funds a portion of the salary and also provides a generous annual stipend to cover expenses for research, travel and scholarly materials.

"(The professorship) will support both teaching and scholarship in the broad range of disciplines usually referred to as 'the Humanities,'" Naylor said. "But its establishment not only contributes to continued academic excellence at the College, it also honors a man of great erudition and refinement, Professor Ralph S. Collins."

Collins

Erica Steffe, in attendance at the recent installation ceremony, shared, in a PowerPoint presentation, the story of her father's life, beginning with his birth in 1910 and including many stories from his, his wife and children's time in Maryville and abroad.

Always considered Maryville 'home'

Displaying a State Department bio sheet that her father had filled out in 1962, Steffe said her father and mother, Maria Zubiller Collins, always considered Maryville, Tenn., their legal residence.

Following his retirement from the College, Steffe said that her father "stayed active at New Providence Presbyterian Church, played golf at Green Meadows, attended Kiwanis meetings and took up hiking in the Smoky Mountains. He enjoyed spending time with his grandchildren and attending concerts and lectures at the College."

Maria passed away in 1992. Ralph stayed active, though decreasing his hiking time in the Smokies. Steffe said her father enjoyed walking the Green Belt trails in Maryville, breaking up his walks with stops at the Blount County Public Library and the College's Lamar Memorial Library.

He passed away in 1998.

"Ralph and Maria are buried in the Maryville College cemetery, at rest on the campus that meant so much to them and in the town that welcomed them and made them feel at home," Steffe said. "As I worked on editing their memoirs, I became increasingly aware of how much Maryville meant to them, and it is to honor Maryville College, as well as Ralph Collins' memory, that I am establishing this professorship."

To read more of Steffe's remarks from the PowerPoint presentation, visit maryville college.edu.

Family members at the dedication of the Dr. Ralph S. Collins Professorship in the Humanities in October 2005. Mary Wagner, Melissa Mann, Randall Collins, Adrian Wagner, Erica and Bill Steffee, Chris Mann, Emily Mann, and Taylor Rose Mann.

Atlantic Ocean.

Date	Ship (or plane)	Departing and Arriving	Ralph	Maria	Erica	Randall	Mary	Melissa
1932 Jun	*S.S. Rotterdam*	New York - Boulogne	x					
1933 Aug	*S.S. Statendam*	Boulogne - New York	x					
1945 Apr	*Sea Wolf*	New York - Southhampton	x					
1946 May	*S.S. Uruguay*	New York - Le Havre		x	x	x	x	
1948 Apr	*S.S. America*	Southhampton - New York	x	x	x	x	x	
1949 Jul	*S.S. Gripsholm*	New York - Göteborg	x	x	x	x	x	
1949 Jul	*Belo-Ostrov*	Stockholm - Helsinki - Leningrad	x	x	x	x	x	
1950 Sep	*S.S. Brynhild*	Helsinki - Stockholm	x	x	x	x	x	
1950 Sep	*M.S. Oslofjord*	Oslo - New York		x	x	x	x	
1951 Jul	*Île de France*	Le Havre - New York	x					
1951 Oct	*Nieuw Amsterdam*	New York - Rotterdam	x	x	x	x	x	x
1954 Jul	*S.S. America*	Bremerhaven - New York	x	x	x	x	x	x
1957 May	*S.S. Constitution*	New York - Algeciras	x					
1957 Aug	*S.S. Constitution*	New York - Algeciras		x			x	x
1958 Jun	Pan American (air)	New York - Madrid			x	x		
1958 Sep	*S.S. United States*	Le Havre - New York			x	x		
1959 Jul	*S.S. Independence*	Barcelona - New York	x	x			x	x
1959 Sep	*S.S. Independence*	New York - Morocco - Barcelona	x	x			x	x
1960 Jun	*Cabo San Vicente*	Barcelona - Montevideo	x	x			x	x
1960 Jun	*S.S. Argentina*	New York - Montevideo			x	x		
1960 Aug	*S.S. Brasil*	Montevideo - New York			x			
1960 Sep	Pan American	Montevideo - New York				x		
1961 Oct	*Delta Del Sud*	Montevideo - New Orleans	x	x			x	x
1962 Jan	Pan American	New York - Montevideo	x	x			x	x
1962 Sep	Pan American	Montevideo - New Orleans					x	
1963 Oct	*S.S. Brasil*	Montevideo - New York	x	x				x

S.S. America leaves New York City in the 1950s and heads south toward the open Atlantic.

Thirty years of ocean crossings

We children loved the travel to and from foreign posts. It generally took two to three weeks to travel from New York to a city like Berlin or Moscow. The first week we were on an ocean liner crossing the Atlantic. Then we continued by train, with a few ferries, cars, and jeeps sandwiched in between.

On our trip to Moscow we traveled with 27 footlockers and trunks, and our job as children was to sit on these containers whenever they were stacked on a pier or on a train station platform while our parents went to check on the tickets, and it was my job to count the luggage.

Erica

Baggage

Ship all heavy baggage to arrive at the steamship pier at least 24 hours before sailing. Always make sure, either by personal observation or proper claim check, that all baggage is going with you. Baggage insurance is strongly recommended.

From the steamship company you can obtain labels which should be pasted on all your baggage. The trunks you will not need on the voyage are marked "Hold." Those needed during the voyage are marked "Wanted" and will be held for you in the ship's baggage room. Your steamer trunks and hand baggage will accompany you to the state-room.

Ship Travel Instructions

Erica and Randall leaving New York on the *Nieuw Amsterdam* in 1951.

Miscellaneous

Travel light. Secure a deck chair when obtaining tickets and arrange that the deck chair is placed on the starboard side of the promenade deck when sailing East, and port side when sailing West. Thus you will be facing South all the time.

Since there are entertainments on board the ship, it is advisable to be prepared for such occasions, especially when fancy dress balls and the like are included.

Ship Travel Instructions

Deck sports

There are many popular deck sports which you may enjoy while on board ship. If you are to enjoy these games, you must enter into them without feeling that it is necessary to have been formally introduced to the participants. Ship's passengers are in a sense "one big family."

Ship Travel Instructions

Above: Melissa on the *Cabo San Vicente*.
Left and below: On the *Nieuw Amsterdam*.

Difference in time	
Amsterdam (Holland)	5.20 p.m.
Berlin (Germany)	5.54 p.m.
Brussels (Belgium)	5.00 p.m.
Calcutta (India)	10.50 p.m.
Cape Town (South Africa)	5.50 p.m.
Chicago	11.00 a.m.
Copenhagen (Denmark)	5.50 p.m.
Cherbourg (France)	5.00 p.m.
London (England)	5.00 p.m.
Madrid (Spain)	4.45 p.m.
Manila (P.I.)	*1.00 a.m.
Melbourne (Australia)	*2.40 p.m.
NEW YORK CITY	12.00 NOON
Paris (France)	5.09 p.m.
Peking (China)	*1.00 a.m.
Leningrad (Russia)	7.01 p.m.
Rome (Italy)	5.50 p.m.
San Francisco	9.00 a.m.
Stockhom (Sweden)	6.12 p.m.
Switzerland	6.00 p.m.
Vienna (Austria)	6.06 p.m.
Yokohama (Japan)	*2.00 a.m.
	* next day

Before time zones were standardized, the time differences among cities were as varied as those on the above chart.

Dad loved ocean voyages for getting from one post to another. He liked changing the clock only one hour each night. And he liked the chance to relax during a crossing that generally took a week or longer. He walked several miles a day on deck and partied at night!

Erica

Above: The *S.S. America*, left, is docked at Bremerhaven. At right is the stern of the *Olympia*.
Top left: Ralph and Melissa on the deck of the *S.S. America* in July 1954.
Lower left: Maria, Randall, Mary, and Ralph arriving at Cobh, Ireland in 1951.

Foreign hotels

When engaging rooms at hotels where there are no printed rates, it is always best to have a definite understanding as to the price per day or week. In Southern Europe when travellers do not bargain for their rooms, they may be overcharged. As a rule, the upper floor rates are more reasonable in price and are often more comfortable due to less street noises and more ventilation.

Avoid extras if possible, especially food, for, unlike America, exorbitant prices are often charged for them. Except for the larger hotels in the capital cities, there are very few rooms with bath. There is usually a bath on each floor. Arrangements may be made at the desk for its use by payment of a slight additional charge. Soap is seldom supplied, and it is best to carry your own.

Ship Travel Instructions

Home was where the family was

Addresses where Ralph Collins lived

1910-1917	Farm outside Grifton, North Carolina
1918-1926	Farm on Jolly Road, outside Ayden, North Carolina
1926-1932	University of North Carolina, Chapel Hill
1932-1933	30 Jägerstrasse, Munich, Germany
1933-1934	Ayden, North Carolina
1934-1935	Wilson, North Carolina
1935-1937	Miller Street, Maryville, Tennessee
1938-1941	103½ High Street, Maryville, Tennessee
1941-1945	518 Clark Street, Maryville, Tennessee (house address became 208 Elm Ave. and is now 208 Clarion Ave.)
1945	Hotel on Cromwell Road, London
1945	Père Vatel quarters, Versailles
1945	Camp Dentine, Kassel, Germany
1945	Marburg, Germany
1945	Mediterraneo & Savoia Hotels, Rome, Italy
1946-1948	4 Am Erlenbusch, Dahlem, Berlin, West Germany
1948	3280 Chestnut Street NW, Washington, DC
1948-1949	Butler Hall, Columbia University, New York City
1949-1950	1st Ostankino Street, Moscow, USSR
1950-1951	16 Vesnina Street, Moscow, USSR
1951	12 Gumpelsheimerstrasse, Regensburg, W. Germany
1952	2 Quellenweg, Bad Homburg, West Germany
1952-1954	14 Joachim Becherstrasse (HICOG Project) Frankfurt-am-Main, West Germany
1954-1957	2753 Woodley Place NW, Washington, DC
1957-1960	2 San Ignacio, piso 3, Algorta, Bilbao, Spain
1960-1962	3074 Avenida Brasil, piso 8, Montevideo, Uruguay
1962-1963	2904 Bulevar Espãna, Montevideo, Uruguay
1963-1967	5253 Nebraska Avenue NW, Washington, DC
1967-1998	1741 Linda Lane, Maryville, Tennessee
1998	Judson Park, Cleveland, Ohio

The family in Dörnbach in 1952.

Because our family moved so frequently during my childhood and adolescence, I didn't really have a place I considered to be "home" apart from wherever we happened to be living at the time. As a result, I associate "home" even now with a person rather than with a place.

Mary

When I was a freshman in college, I listed my home as Bilbao. "Home" is wherever my family happened to be living. When someone asks me where I'm from, I answer, "I grew up in Europe."

During my four years in college I saw my parents and sisters once a year. Randy and I flew to Spain for summer vacation in 1958. Dad brought the family back from Spain on home leave in the summer of 1959. Randy and I took an ocean liner from New York City to Montevideo for summer vacation in 1960. And we saw the family in December 1961 when Dad had home leave and the family came to Cornwall-on-Hudson for Christmas! During our school breaks we stayed either with our grandparents or with classmates. We worked at odd jobs or traveled, in my case by bus.

Erica

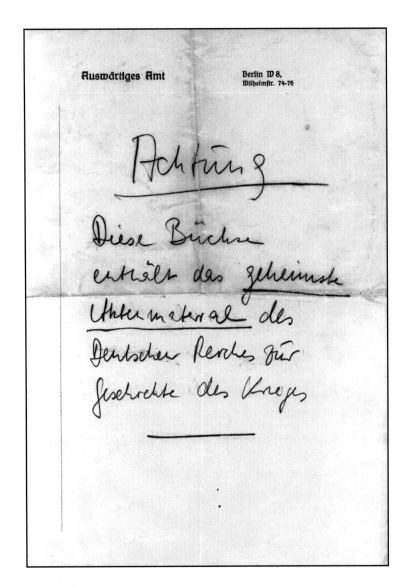

Auswärtiges Amt

Berlin W 8,
Wilhelmstr. 74-76

Achtung

Diese Büchse
enthält das geheimste
Uhtermaterial des
Deutschen Reiches zur
Geschichte des Krieges

[German] Foreign Office   Berlin
<u>Attention</u>
These canisters contain the <u>top-secret documents</u> of the
German Reich regarding affairs of war.

Top secret.

Opposite is a montage of the Molotov-Ribbentrop Pact, with the signatures of Ribbentrop (Germany) and Molotov (Russia).

The four pages that follow are a photostat of the report filed in 1945 by British Lieutenant Colonel Robert Thomson, who, with Ralph Collins, unearthed the Pact.

NICHTANGRIFFSVERTRAG ZWISCHEN DEUTSCHLAND UND DER UNION DER SOZIALISTISCHEN SOWJETREPUBLIKEN.

Die Deutsche Reichsregierung
die Regierung der Un'
Sowjetrepubliken
geleitet
zwischen De
gehend

...einander bleiben, um sich gege
...formieren, die ihre gemeinsamen Intere

Artikel IV.

Keiner der beiden vertragschliessenden Te
sich an irgend einer Mächtegruppierung beteiligen,
unmittelbar oder unmittelbar gegen den anderen Teil rio

Artikel V.

Falls Streitigkeiten oder Konflikte zwischen den
Vertragschliessenden Teilen über Fragen dieser oder jener
Art entstehen sollten, werden beide Teile diese Streitig-
keiten oder Konflikte ausschliesslich auf dem Wege freund-
schaftlichen Meinungsaustausches oder nötigenfalls durch
Einsetzung von Schlichtungskommissionen bereinigen.

Artikel VI.

Der gegenwärtige Vertrag wird auf di
Jahren abgeschlossen mit der Maa
einer der Vertragschlie-
lauf dieser F
die

...ne Reichsregierung:

In Vollmacht
der Regierung
der UdSSR

Moskau am 23. August 1939.

Discovery of Secret Archives of German Foreign Ministry.

On May 12 I was in Muehlhausen (Thuringia) for the purpose of examining certain Foreign Ministry archives. By a fortunate coincidence I ran into Dr. Ralph Collins, of the State Department, a member of the U. S. Team working in the closest collaboration with my own. We remained together for four days, during which time Dr. Collins' presence was not only helpful in emphasising the co-operation existing between our two countries, but his counsel and companionship were invaluable in the unusual experiences which I am about to describe.

While returning alone from an interview with a German Foreign Ministry key man, I was approached by a man of some 30 years of age who, speaking faultless English, asked me to convey to London a letter addressed to Mr. Duncan Sandys, the British Minister for Housing and son-in-law of Mr. Winston Churchill. It transpired later that the man had no idea that I was searching for the very things which he was willing to reveal, but merely spoke to me because I was a British officer, a somewhat rare specimen in Thuringia. I told him that I could not undertake to forward the letter without some idea of the contents, whereupon the man said that I might read what he had written. I did so, and found that the writer (Herr Carl von LOESCH), a former fellow-student with Mr. Sandys, offered to disclose to the latter the whereabouts of a set of microfilms of 30 boxes of the most top secret German Foreign Ministry papers, containing a complete account of Germany's foreign policy and doings from 1933 to 1944, and including correspondence and records of conversations between Hitler and Ribbentrop on the one side and Mussolini, Franco, Laval, Molotov and Japanese and other personalities on the other, also reports by ambassadors and ministers on the most secret matters. Herr von Loesch was the understudy of the well-known Dr. Schmidt and interpreted at many meetings between Hitler and foreign statesmen. He was sent to Thuringia last February to house and look after the most secret archives. Owing to the sudden Allied advance orders were received to destroy the collection. This was done, but not before a set of microfilms was retrieved and buried in a lonely spot. The writer of the letter asked to be transferred with two assistants to British-occupied territory and put into touch with a Foreign Office representative with a view to the printing, sorting and rebuilding of the complete mass of films in rolls, at present in disorder. Von Loesch asked to be allowed to undertake the work, which would have to be done in Great Britain, and produced a British passport as evidence of his British nationality by birth in London.

The man emphasised his desire to deal with the British rather than the Americans, whereupon I stated that although a Foreign Office official I also represented the State Department because we Allies were working in complete collaboration. There could be no question of a separate deal with one government. I would report the matter to the U.S. military authorities, as representing the interests of both Allies, because they were in occupation of the area. He would be informed of their decision. Dr. Collins was not present at the talk but collaborated fully in all that followed.

We decided to lay the matter the next day before the 1st Army G. 2 at Weimar and to ask for their approval to negotiate with the man for the unearthing of the films and their transfer with him to our HQ at

at the castle in Marburg/Lahn, which is well within American-occupied
territory, whereas Thuringia is shortly due to be taken over by the
Russians. At Weimar we found no G. 2 Section because the 1st Army had
moved out and the 9th Army had not yet arrived. We managed to speak,
however, with more than one responsible officer who, while disclaiming
responsibility, voiced the opinion that we should go ahead and report ~~late~~
later.

Accordingly on Monday, May 14, we motored to a village situated some
20 miles from Muehlhausen in order to see our man. I went alone into the
house, leaving Dr. Collins with the driver of the jeep. I told von Loesch
that I was prepared, on receiving to remove them and him to Marburg ~~Cast~~
Castle, where he could restore the prints to order so that the whole
would form a series of connected narratives. I could not agree to the
transfer of his two assistants whose help he considered essential. The
action taken would be reported to the allied authorities for a definitive
decision as to his ultimate treatment. I emphasised that he would be
treated with consideration and would certainly not starve at Marburg, but
that I was only empowered to make a promise covering the immediate future.
He enquired whether he would be regarded as a prisoner of war, to which I
replied in the negative and promised that he would be subjected to no
indignities but only to the same restrictions on liberty as Germans in
general. He would naturally be under surveillance while dealing with the
secret files. After a few more enquiries on his part I said that if he
dealt honourably with me he could count on a like attitude on my part.
He then accepted my conditions.

As a precaution I then invited Herr von Loesch to accompany me to the
jeep, where in Dr. Collins' presence I summarised the arrangements made,
again stressing the fact that it related to the immediate future only.
Once more the man signified his acceptance.

We then proceeded some four miles by jeep to the neighbourhood of a
large country house named Schoeneberg in which a detachment of the 5th
Armoured Division was quartered. I presented my army clearance papers
at the house and asked that a representative of the U. S. army might
accompany us to the site of the alleged buried treasure. Ready compliance
was expressed by Captain Albert M. Folkard who, bearing arms, accompanied
Dr. Collins, Herr von Loesch and myself along a private path in the estate
to a point where we had to descend, rather uncomfortably, a steep ravine
banked with pine trees. Our guide halted at a certain spot where he and
Captain Folkard with iron bars soon scraped the soil from a waterproof
cape covering a large can. This Captain Folkard brought to the top of the
declivity and placed under guard in the mansion. He promised to submit
to the colonel the request of von Loesch for the release of his automobile
stored at an adjoining farm.

Dr. Collins and I then proceeded to Muehlhausen with Herr von Loesch.
We had no difficulty in obtaining a pass for the latter's journey with
his own automobile in our convoy to Marburg. We also reported the find
to the C. I. C. of the Military Government and that of the Army Division,
both of which scrutinised my papers, a step quite properly requested by
telephone by Captain Folkard.

On our return to Schoeneberg Dr. Collins and I gladly accepted the hospitality of Colonel Douglas Page, Commanding Div. Artillery, 5th Armoured
Division, to be his guests overnight. Colonel Page has that rare spirit

of genuine hospitality which left two tired and jaded travellers with
the impression that their visit had been a genuine pleasure to him.
There was not one of his officers who did not second Col. Page's efforts
to make us thoroughly at home. Meanwhile Captain Folkard continued to
be responsible for the can of unassuming appearance but presumably
valuable contents. Von Loesch we had sent home and arranged to pick up
on the following day.

On Tuesday, May 15, we proceeded to Muehlhausen with Captain
Folkard and reported all the facts to Lt.-Col. MacFarland of the Army
Division C. I. C. On returning to Schoeneberg we had the honour of
meeting Major-General Oliver, Commanding 5th Armoured Division, who was
good enough to give general approval to our proceedings and to our acting
at our discretion.

After lunch we proceeded in convoy to Marburg via Dentine Camp.
Colonel Page had considerately provided an M. 40 armed car for our find
and for the luggage of our growing party. In addition he released
without demur the car of Herr von Loesch and provided petrol for its
use. Captain Folkard continued to be personally responsible for guard-
ing the can. At Dentine we met our own R.A.F. microfilming unit and for
the first time, with the help of their magnifying reading apparatus,
formed a first-hand idea of the value of the unearthed films. They
fully correspond to the informant's description and will undoubtedly
supply information of immense value which may not be obtainable elsewhere. Our technicians advised us that they could undertake the printing work if equipment and paper could be made available in Germany,
which ought to be the case, but eventually, in view of transport and
communication difficulties, we decided unanimously that the best plan
was for me to to proceed to London, get the Air Ministry to make
prints and return with them to Marburg for sorting etc.

On the value of the find being thus confirmed Dr. Collins and I
decided to get Herr von Loesch's assistants (a man and a woman) brought
to Marburg lest the Russians should put pressure on them to make disclosures . Rumours are already in circulation, as witness para. 8 of
a memorandum dated April 30 by Mr. H. B. Morris to AC of S, G. 2 Shaef,
Goldcup HQ. Captain Folkard is accordingly arranging to bring the
two individuals soon to Marburg. They will be installed in an apartment in the castle, where Herr von Loesch already is.

The man is making interesting disclosures and is quite willing to
talk about his relations with Hitler and others. I have been able to
check up on some of his statements and have found them remarkably
accurate. He says, for instance, that months ago the Gestapo supplied
the German Foreign Ministry with copies of the Instrument of Surrender
and of the Agreement for the Division of Germany into Zones of Allied
Occupation (with maps), both of which I have seen. His description of
the details is extremely like my remembrance of them. I have requested
Team members to make memoranda of his statements of interest. The man
may be an opportunist but he quite accepts the situation that he is in
our power and to my mind seems quite prepared to be useful to us in
the interests of his own future. His Germany has gone for ever and he
is quite willing to adjust himself to a new state of affairs. I am
seeing that he is treated with courtesy and consideration but without
tenderness, and needless to say he is under strict surveillance.

Dr. Collins' sound judgment and common-sense were of the utmost
value

T O P/S E C R E T

value in handling a delicate and unexpected situation and we both derived
pleasure in demonstrating, in a variety of places, the identity of interests
of our governments and despatching agencies. Next to him merit is due to Cap
Captain Folkard for the ungrudging assistance so readily rendered in looking
after our treasure trove and in convoying it over a drive of many hours. He
was constantly solicitous for our comfort and for the safety of his charge,
and both Dr. Collins and I feel that we must pay a warm tribute to him.

R.G. Thomson, Lt. Col.

Leader of Foreign Office Field Team, Item 28 of C.I.O.S.
Black List.

Distribution:-

Copies to -
Documents Control Section, 12th Army Group (documents cleared
Documents Section, 9th Army.   through them).
Documents Section, Shaef (documents cleared through them).
G. 2, 9th Army.
C.I.C., MUelhausen (Thuringia).
Captain Folkard, A.P.O. 255, U.S. Forces.
G. 2, Economic Section, Shaef.
C.I.O.S., London.
G. 2, 12th Army Group.
G. 2, Economic Section, 12th Army Group.
Mr. Donald Heath, Shaef (Main).
Dr. Perkins, U. S. Embassy, London (Leader of State Dept. Field
                                    Team).

T O P S E C R E T

Winston Churchill at the memorial service for President Roosevelt, at St. Paul's Cathedral, in April 1945.

Ralph Collins witnessing history

Ralph was frequently on the spot where major historical events happened, and he personally met or saw many important world leaders.

This list includes the highlights of his diplomatic career.

Nazi book-burning in 1932.

Adolf Hitler.

Seeing Adolf Hitler frequently on the balcony of his Munich headquarters in 1932-33, and hearing his last speech before the election in 1933.

Witnessing Nazi book-burning in Munich in 1932.

Hearing Benito Mussolini's speech in Rome in 1933.

Seeing Winston Churchill at the memorial service for President Roosevelt in London in 1945.

Witnessing the Nuremberg trials of Nazi war criminals in 1946.

Mussolini addressing a crowd.

Nuremberg trial.

Nikita Khrushchev.

John Foster Dulles (right) and Adenauer.

Seeing Joseph Stalin on official occasions in Moscow during 1949-51.

Seeing Nikita Khrushchev, the Soviet Premier, at a party at the US Embassy in Moscow in 1955.

Briefing Secretary of State John Foster Dulles numerous times during the 1950s.

Meeting Generalíssimo Francisco Franco, the Spanish dictator, on a visit to Bilbao in 1959.

Meeting President Eisenhower on his visit to Spain in 1960.

Generalíssimo Franco.

Eisenhower (right).

Pope John XXIII.

Dean Rusk.

Seeing Pope John XXIII at a public appearance in 1960, when Ralph took Mary on a trip to Italy.

Meeting President John F. Kennedy on his visit to the Punta del Este Conference in Uruguay in 1962.

Briefing Secretary of State Dean Rusk on various occasions during the 1960s.

Meeting Senator Robert F. Kennedy, Secretary of Defense Robert McNamara, and Ambassador Averill Harriman when they spoke at the National Interdepartmental Seminar in the 1960s.

President Kennedy and Robert McNamara.

Robert Kennedy.

To explore further

Amerika magazine is found in University libraries with US Government Document Depositories.

Bissonnette, Rev. Georges, *Moscow was My Parish*, McGraw Hill, 1956.

Cherny, Andrei, *The Candy Bombers: the Untold Story of the Berlin Airlift and America's Finest Hour,* G.P. Putnam's Sons, 2008

Collins, Maria and Ralph, *Life in a Dacha, An American Family in Moscow*, 1949-1950, self-published, 2003.

Gilmore, Eddy, *Me and My Russian Wife*, Doubleday, 1954.

Hixson, Walter L., *Parting the Curtain; Propoganda, Culture, and the Cold War, 1945-1961*, St. Martin's Press, 1997.

Kirk, Lydia Chapin, *Distinguished Service, Partner in Diplomacy*, Syracuse University Press, 2007.

Kurlansky, Mark, *The Basque History of the World*, Walker Publishing Company, 1999.

Molotov-Ribbontrop Pact, 1939, National Archives, Washington DC, Microfilm T120, Roll 616, Frames F110048-50.

Montefiore, Simon Sebag, *The Court of the Red Tsar*, Knopf, 2004.

Montefiore, Simon Sebag, *Young Stalin*, Knopf, 2007.

Murphy, Robert, *Diplomat Among Warriors; the unique world of a Foreign Service expert*, Doubleday, 1964.

Steinbeck, John, *A Russian Journal*, Viking Press, 1948.

The worldwide web, including Wikipedia, offers a wealth of information and photographs.

Index of features